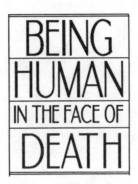

BEING
HUMAN
IN THE FACE OF
DEATH

BEING
HUMAN
IN THE FACE OF
DEATH

EDITED BY
DEBORAH ROTH, M.S.C.
EMILY LeVIER, M.S.C.

IBS PRESS
Santa Monica, CA

Cover photo copyright by Melvin L. Harris
Cover design by Melvin L. Harris and Susan C. Muller-Harris
Book design and type composition by Susan C. Muller-Harris
Copyediting by Laura Norvig and Miriam Jacobson

IBS PRESS
744 Pier Avenue
Santa Monica, CA 90405
(213) 450-6485

IBS PRESS FIRST PRINTING, JANUARY 1990

Library of Congress Cataloging in Publication Data
Roth, Deborah
   Being human in the face of death / edited by Deborah Roth & Emily Levier.
      p.   cm.
   Includes bibliographical references (p.   ).
   ISBN 0-9616605-8-9 : $9.95
      1. Terminal care--Psychological aspects.   2. Death--Psychological aspects.
3. Helping behavior--Psychological aspects.   I. Levier, Emily.   II. Title.
R726.8.R68   1990
362.1'75--dc20   89-28330
                                                                            CIP

ISBN 0-9616605-8-9

Manufactured in the United States of America

To H.S. with Gratitude.
Fall, 1989

CONTENTS

2 CARING FOR THE CAREGIVER

3 OTHER DIMENSIONS OF DEATH

4 THE CAREGIVER'S WORKBOOK

INTRODUCTION

By Mary Ball

M**ARY BALL** *is the founder of The Center for Help in Time of Loss, a thriving community center which offers a multitude of specialized support groups as well as accredited training programs for nurses. All of the contributors to this book have worked with The Center for Help in Time of Loss in some capacity, and they refer to it in their essays as simply, "the center." For more information please contact:*

The Center for Help in Time of Loss
326 Hillsdale Avenue
Hillsdale, NJ 07642
(201)666-0009

The purpose of this book is to help caregivers who work with dying people unlock one of the best resources they have—their humanness. After more than ten years of working with terminal patients and their families, and providing training courses for professionals and volunteers in this field, we have come to believe that the most significant question to be explored is: How can we stay open, vulnerable, compassionate—all that being human implies, and still retain our professionalism? This has always been a dilemma in health care, but perhaps nowhere is this more acute than when we care for dying people.

In medical training the emphasis is, of course, on saving lives. Death is seen as the enemy. Even the most experienced nurses who come to the center for training courses seem unprepared to work with dying patients. This also seems to hold true for many doctors and clergy as well. The problem does not stem simply from schooling, but is the result of a much more pervasive issue: our fear of the unknown, our fear of death.

To be present for another person without imposing one's own beliefs, expectations, and without having any answers to give, requires a genuine inner clarity. Perhaps no other area of caregiving demands more self-honesty than that of working with dying patients and their families. This is not to devalue the need for concepts, theories and practical methods. In fact, the objectivity of a professional is vital when family and friends are caught up in their own emotions and are often unable to relate to the dying person's needs.

Being able to facilitate communication between patient and family members can be one of the caregiver's major contributions, and a skill that requires training for mastery. What this book is about is finding the balance that allows us to be cool-headed and warm-hearted while confronting the most profound mystery we human beings face.

When we started the Center for Help in Time of Loss in 1978, our aim was to ease the stress and isolation for people going through catastrophic illness, and to help families through death and bereavement. We wanted to create a safe place where dying people and their families could find their own answers without being given advice or being told how they should feel. What began as a single support group trained by Dr. Elisabeth Kübler-Ross, evolved into a home-care program, a counseling department specializing in grief and loss, eleven different support groups, including one for caregivers, and a training program on caring for the terminally ill. From our experience, we decided that the most essential tool we could offer other caregivers is a way to overcome the blocks that keep us from relating to people with an open mind and an open heart.

The professionals who share their experience in this book have found their own unique ways for remaining human in the face of death. They discuss some of the difficult issues they faced, and offer suggestions which will help you care for others with renewed awareness.

Although the advice they offer is geared toward helping those who have made caregiving their profession, it is equally valuable for those who are caring for a loved one at home.

We have also included a workbook section derived from the center's eight-week training course that is designed to help caregivers focus on their attitudes and determine what, if any, are their own obstacles and how to deal with them.

While compiling the stories in this book, we began to see that there were certain characteristics that were keys to successful caregiving. We have also included a section on Caring for the Caregiver, which we consider one of the most significant aspects of work with the terminally ill. Without self-nurturing, the caregiver will have little left to give others.

There is something else we have discovered that is worth mentioning, too. Those who choose to work with dying patients and their families will find a surprising exchange usually takes place—the gifts they bring to others are given to themselves.

EIGHT KEYS TO SUCCESSFUL CAREGIVING

- To Be Totally Present
- To Offer Hope and Respect
- To Hear With the Heart
- To Be Authentic and Flexible
- To Seek Self-Honesty
- To Cultivate Response-Ability
- To Keep an Open Mind
- To Journey Side By Side

JUST BEING

The art of "just being" is the only must for the caring profession.

It is complete involvement with the patient without the need to impose any of your own words or advice; trivia or observations.

The art of "just being" involves your head and your heart.

Wisdom and love of man are intertwined so that the patient can respond as he wishes with the knowledge that someone cares enough to give of their time and self and expects nothing in return.

While you make no demands of the patient, you do derive the satisfaction that you met this patient according to his needs and, for that brief period, all that existed between you was love and understanding.

—DONNA D. BETTES

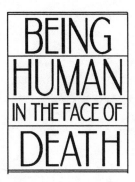

BEING
HUMAN
IN THE FACE OF
DEATH

Part 1

The Keys to Successful Caregiving

1

BEING FULLY PRESENT

By Charles Lochner, M.A., M.S.

C HARLES LOCHNER *is coordinator of counseling services for
The Center for Help in Time of Loss. Lochner has taught
classes on death and dying for nurses and other professionals for more than fifteen years. A composer and songwriter,
he uses his own music to help patients, families and caregivers
unlock their feelings. His unique gifts as a counselor and teacher
have been internationally acclaimed. His work has been funded
for the past three years by the Robert F. Wood Johnson Foundation.*

Before I get into the subject of caring for the terminally
ill, I'd like to tell you a story that is key to what we're really
dealing with in this book. No matter what you take away
after reading this in terms of facts and data, it's not nearly
as important as what goes on inside of you—inside of me—

when we go to care for others. The fact is that nothing shakes us more profoundly than the issues surrounding death and dying. And the major illusion for caregivers is that somehow we're talking about someone else. *Someone else* is sick; *someone else* is dying; and it is *someone else* who is losing a loved one. This is not about me, we think. Yet, the secret of caring in this specific area is that it really is about all of us. One of the things we need to confront whenever we deal with death and loss is our own denial. I'll mention more about that later, but now I want to tell you my story. It's a parable to help situate us.

In a certain town there lived a man who was known as the wisest man in the world. No matter what anyone would ask him, he could come up with the right answer. He never missed. There also lived in this same town another person who didn't like the fact that someone had the answer to everything, and so he set out to prove him wrong. He thought if he could find some sort of trick question, he could make the wise man wrong no matter how he answered. He thought and thought, and finally he had it. He would place a bird in his hands and ask, "Wise man, is the bird in my hands alive or dead?" If the wise man answered "alive," he would crush the bird, and if he answered "dead," he would open his hands and let the bird fly free. So he found the wise man one day, and with the bird in his hand, he said, "Oh Wise One, I've heard so much about you since I was little. They say that you can answer any question. Tell me then, is the bird in my hands alive or dead?" The wise man thought for a long time and then he replied, "My dear young man, whether the bird in your hands is alive or dead I do not know, but this much I do know, the answer to your question lies in your own hands."

After you read all the books, finish all the workshops, go for all the training, all the schooling, you still have to confront death. Both your own and others'. The task is to look within ourselves. To pay attention to our own lives, our own suffering, our own daily dying. Without doing this, we cannot be fully present with someone. Without owning our own pain we will be frightened by the pain of others. We will push it away. We will push them away.

Unfortunately, many professional caregivers leave their most valuable asset behind when they go to the bedside of a dying person or when they see a person who is grieving. That most valuable asset is their own life and the experience of their own brokenness. Without this component, these well-intentioned, highly educated people simply become technicians. However, people who go through such a crisis don't want technicians, they want people. They want people who can be there, who can take their stand in that space. In order to do that, there's an awful lot of personal processing we have to tend to inside ourselves. We have to look at our own fears and at the way we confront the mystery of death. That's not the easiest thing in the world to do. And sometimes it's more difficult for those of us who are helpers. All of us need to do our own homework.

The major difficulty we face, and one that we share with so many people in our own culture, is something we call denial. In other words, it's the illusion that someone else is going to die, not me. Those of you who have worked in this area for a little bit of time know how strong that denial can be. It's pervasive. And it's the denial that death has anything to do with us that prevents us from doing anything about it. You can stay aloof from it, but if you're not in contact with it, then it's difficult to be present for other people in the way that's necessary. We happen to live in a culture that doesn't know what to do with what doesn't work out. When things don't work out, we tend to put them out of our sight. Anyone who doesn't fit into our well ordered understanding of the world, we exclude. In his book *The Pursuit of Loneliness*, sociologist Philip Slater uses the term "the toilet assumption" to describe this phenomenon—that unwanted matter is simply flushed away. It's evident in our patterns of housing, or the way in which we deal with people who have specific illnesses. It's highly visible with AIDS. "It can't happen here!" is the prevailing sentiment. Our traditional mental hospitals are usually these great big places in the country somewhere. Everybody knows what it is, but you don't live near it unless you work there. The same thing with a prison. We don't do much more beyond excluding these groups from our sight.

A number of years ago when we were in the Vietnam war, a senator from Vermont advised us to solve our impasse by declaring a victory, and then getting out. Americans can live with victory; they don't know how to live with loss. It's deeply inbred in our culture, and whenever we have to deal with anything that touches us with loss, or that we understand to be failure in any way, we tend to remove it or let somebody else take care of it. It's the same way we deal with the housing crisis today. We go to meetings and say the government has to do something about the problem, or somebody's got to do something about the homeless, but not in our neighborhood. Someplace else. Out of sight, out of mind. Oftentimes, that is how we live.

We see this at the center in terms of death and dying. We've been around since 1978 and yet many people don't even know we exist, although there's a big sign out front. We usually refer to it as The Center for Help. The name is really The Center for Help in Time of Loss. But if you say loss it scares too many people away. Recently, a woman whose daughter had just died, was introducing me to someone else. "This is Mr. Lochner," she said. "He's from The Center for Help in Time of Loss." Then she added, "Oh, what a terrible name." That's the problem. Loss isn't supposed to be recognized. But when you are dealing with someone who is dying, it's going to be very painful and difficult to ignore loss. Because who do we talk to if what is happening is not acknowledged? Who does the dying person talk to when somebody's trying to talk them out of it?

Culturally there's a problem even giving a workshop or writing a book on the subject. What's the problem? Different forms of denial. How can you explore something if it doesn't exist? We don't even say the word. We spell it. D-E-A-T-H. I remember being with a parent when she was talking about the death of a grandparent around her five-year-old, and she began spelling out the letters of the words D-E-A-T-H, D-Y-I-N-G, F-U-N-E-R-A-L. That creates more anxiety for the child of course. Because children don't pay attention to words so much; they pay attention to feelings. As you may know, when people become ill, they often regress and begin to operate more on feeling. What they sense within the caregiver becomes important. That's why it's not a matter of having all the right information. It's a matter of taking care of your own heart.

An example of total denial was illustrated by the *Christian Science Monitor*'s old policy that the word "death" couldn't be mentioned in its publications. There's also something called denial of the harshness of death. Sometimes the language surrounding the person who died tells you something. People don't die, they "pass away," they "pass on," they "pass out," they "expire." What do you do with that? In Jessica Mitford's classic, *The American Way of Death*, she describes how the deceased is viewed in the "slumber room." They're not dead, they're sleeping. That is, until you go up and touch them, then they're a little cool. Most people don't do that anyway.

It is denial that prevents us from helping, prevents us from being there. This denial is very different than the kind of denial Dr. Elisabeth Kübler-Ross talks about. That's a clinical stage when people try to come to grips with their own death and dying. But there's another cultural form of denial that's quite insidious. Look at what you see on television. People will say we don't deny death, it's all around us. Turn on the television, it's there. It's in almost every major program. They're right! But it's not what you see, it's what you don't see. You don't see a family a year down the road, feeling as if it just happened. You don't see a person struggling with how they are to live their life now that someone they loved is no longer with them. It's not in the script. We don't see the terrible up and down process of grieving.

When someone comes in to see me and I ask if they had a good day, they say, "I don't have good days. I have bad and worse." That's a person talking out of suffering. Sometimes a person will say, "I thought I was doing so well and now I've slipped back." That goes with the territory. We don't see that on TV. No wonder that when it strikes us, it disables us. It's only natural that when we come to deal with the issues around death, our responses are clouded by our denial. When a person comes to us in their grief, we may be tempted to say, "C'mon, what do you think this is? Life goes on." When we say things like that we simply reveal that we do not understand. Only people who go through certain experiences know how to be with, and what to say to, other people. If you've lived a number of years, you've had your losses. Everybody has. I'm sure if we took the time to tell how it is with us in our lives, we would have our stories. All of us. You see, we've all had these experiences, but because of our denial sometimes we haven't tended to them. We haven't looked at them because they're so frightening. And it is because we haven't tended to them that we end up saying the wrong thing.

A number of years ago, when I started doing this work, I taught in a nursing school in Connecticut. We started the course because there was a problem with the staff in the hospital, and with the nurses in particular. When a terminal patient wasn't expected to get out of the hospital, the staff treated them differently and in a negative way. That person wasn't talked to as much as other patients were. People didn't spend the same amount of time with that person as the other patients. That person would be put into a room down at the end of the hall and would be isolated.

A great deal of the problem had to do with the staff's own fears, because in going into that room they saw themselves. That was the hardest thing to deal with, and the crucial thing to deal with, so we started a course. Everybody was very excited about it in the beginning. But after the first two or three sessions, I noticed a type of depression came over them. I thought maybe it was me and the way I was teaching it. It turned out that it had nothing to do with me. It's just that people can't deal with this subject without being reminded of what they've been through, of their own stories. What they need, and what we all need, is to know that no matter how uncomfortable we become, the pain is ultimately friendly. In other words, the task is to move into it and not away from it. I often ask my clients, "Does the pain own you, or do you own the pain?" This process is not about getting rid of the pain. It's about taking ownership. It's about making room in one's life for the pain. Allowing it to be.

You may be thinking, How am I ever going to do this? It's hard for me to be there with someone who's going through this—I'm probably more of a hindrance than a help. Well, I have developed a whole new concept called the "bubble gum theory," meaning that every person that we see, even ones who seem to have it together, are patched up with bubble gum inside—all of us! Nobody has gotten it right! Nobody's that together!

We can't let all of our junk, all of our jumble keep us from being with someone. One of the things that's hardest about relationships is that they're messy. Life just isn't that neat. Once we accept that, then we can make friends and make peace with everything that's a part of us, including our own denial and our own feelings of anger. We are bound to struggle with the loss of somebody that we have been taking care of for a long time. Maybe when we go out of there, we kick the wall because it seems so unfair. We have to make friends with those feelings.

We learn we can't manage a person's life, we are just company for each other along the way. We can't fix it. Nobody has the answers. As soon as you try to come up with one, you've said too much. You've said something that you don't know. It all begins with us. You know the story. "The answer to the question lies within your own hands."

I'd like to tell another little parable for anybody who is still in denial. It seems that a master sent his servant into the marketplace to buy provisions for the day. The servant went into the marketplace, and when he got there, he turned around and saw the figure of Death staring at him. He became so frightened that he ran out of the marketplace and back to his master. "Master," he said, "I was in the marketplace today and I saw Death staring at me. Give me a horse so that I might go away into the desert and escape Death." So the master gave him a horse and he went away to the desert. That afternoon the master himself went to the marketplace and he, too, saw the figure of Death standing there. So he went up to Death and said, "You know, my servant was here this morning and you frightened him so much. Why? Why did you frighten him?" And Death replied, "I did not mean to frighten him, but when I saw him here I was startled. I did not expect to see him here because tonight I have an appointment with him in the desert."

It's about us! Just because we deal with death professionally, and I include myself here very much, doesn't mean we're not playing our own little game, imagining that we are somehow immortal or immune, that it won't happen to us.

To be present for someone else demands that I be present for myself. In order to be company for someone's journey I need to be good company for myself. It means embracing my denial and my fear, accepting myself as I am with love and compassion. Only this self-acceptance will allow me to enter the space of someone else's grief.

We learn to be present for ourselves by taking the time to be quiet. There is no great secret to accomplishing this task. Practice the discipline of quiet and private reflection. Learn to be still, for, in stillness we can meet and befriend ourselves. Quite simply, we must find a quiet place and quiet time where we can put away the books and other paraphernalia of learning and simply listen to our own thoughts and feelings. It is in this time and place that we ultimately discover the power of being present. It is within this place that we discover how to be present with others. Solitude spent in this way purifies the heart for loving and caring. It is really very simple. Death and dying, loving and caring are not new experiences. Although we talk about the hindrances presented by our culture, people have been doing the work of dying and loving very well for centuries. We can learn from those who have done it well. Remember, the answer lies in your own hands. Do not be afraid to take that journey within.

2

HOPE
AND RESPECT

By Julie Dombal, R.N.

JULIE DOMBAL *is an experienced hospice nurse who served as home-care coordinator for The Center for Help in Time of Loss and has led a training program for caregivers.*

No discussion on caring for terminally ill patients would be complete without mentioning the pioneer in the field, Dr. Elisabeth Kübler-Ross. As you may know, she was originally a Swiss psychiatrist who, in 1965, was working at a hospital in Chicago, when a group of theological students came to her asking to speak to someone who was dying. Kübler-Ross went around on one of the floors to look for a dying patient, and much to her surprise, in this hospital it seemed that no one was dying. The problem was that nobody, be it doctors, nurses, whoever, would identify any of their patients as someone who was dying.

Finally, she did locate someone who would allow her and her students to talk to one of these patients who was admittedly terminal. She said she and her students would be back the next day, but when they did return, the dying man was too weak to speak to them. This gave her the opportunity to learn that when someone is willing to talk about it, you must seize the moment. You can't wait until it's convenient for you.

Sometimes you might not feel that you are the appropriate one for this person to talk to. You may be a social worker and feel that a counselor would do a better job. But from my experience, if a person feels comfortable with you, and if you can allow this to happen, you'll get more than you'd realize.

From her many conversations with dying people, Kübler-Ross formulated a theory that she labeled "the five stages of dying." These are common stages that most people seem to go through in their dying. They are really coping mechanisms that we all use for losses of many kinds—all the losses that we've been through in our lives. As I go through them you'll certainly recognize them. It can be very helpful in dealing with people who have catastrophic illnesses to be aware of the ways they deal with what is happening. It is unwise, I believe, to attempt to take these coping mechanisms from them, however bizarre or absurd their behavior may seem. Usually this is how a person has been coping all his or her life.

■ DENIAL

Denial is a buffer for a lot of people. Many times when you tell someone bad news, the first thing they say is "I can't believe it." Not her, not them. They're too young;

they're too old. There are a thousand reasons why it can't be. It's a very common reaction to even the smallest bad news. As a buffer it gives us a little more time to let the bad news in. It gives us time to mobilize our other defense mechanisms, to gather a little bit of information. Some people choose denial all their lives. I happen to be one of them. I used to be a hospice nurse, and I found that some people want to know what they can expect when they are dying. The families want to know so that when things happen, they won't be so afraid. I would always ask people if they wanted to know what was going to happen. I remember one man who said he wanted to know. He was the father of the family. He wanted to know exactly what was going to happen, but only the good news. I respected his wishes. Many people use denial selectively.

A patient may sense from parents, friends or lovers the unspoken message, Don't talk to me about death. The spoken words might be, "Stop feeling sorry for yourself," or "Don't worry, you'll be fine." Or it might be conveyed through body language or a look. But they get the message that they should not talk about their dying, and they don't.

You often hear a mixed message when one member of the family says, "He knows exactly what's happening to him," and another will say, "What are you talking about? He's planning to go on a cruise two years from now, and he's still saving his money for the trip." Some people go in and out of denial. It's easier for them to cope with an illness if they don't have to face it every minute of the day. It might seem totally unrealistic, buying that winter coat when they won't be here next year to wear it, but it allows people to go through every day, be it a minute or an hour, without the stress of the situation. For you as a caregiver it can be very frustrating. You want them to write their will; you want to help them make concrete plans that will help the survivors, and they won't, because they are NOT dying. It's tough. But still, you can't take their denial away and leave them nothing in its place.

■ ANGER

After denial, you may see anger as a coping mechanism. Reality has filtered through. They're thinking, It's true, it's happening to me, why me? I'm only twenty-three, thirty-three, eighty-three, why me? Why not so-and-so? I've taken care of terminally ill patients for the past five years, why me?

When people are first diagnosed with an illness, they may look well, feel well, and they can support a fantasy type of approach to the illness. But when they become thinner, lose their hair or show other outward symptoms that people start to question, then denial breaks down. When anger sets in, it can take the form of envy, rage or resentment.

Patients in the hospital often get angry at workers who come and complain because they got stuck in traffic. The dying person would love to get stuck in a traffic jam. Instead, he's stuck in a hospital. Anger can be displaced in many directions, and a lot of times it's displaced onto the caregiver. It's not easy when you're the target for anger. I try to place myself in their position. What if all of a sudden I couldn't work, or was stigmatized by people around me?

I remember a man I worked for who was unable to get out by himself. He couldn't drive. He sat in his kitchen all day by himself looking out the window of his apartment enraged at a person who would drive up and be able to get out of his car and walk.

Often when the family is the target for the anger, they stop coming to visit the sick person. So the patient becomes more isolated and more angry. People who are catastrophically ill and dealing with anger need to know they are going to be cared for. Sometimes the anger is a way of getting attention. What they really need is to receive attention without having to be angry to get it. They need to know that they will be allowed to function for as long as they can and at the highest level they can.

The word "terminal" can sometimes cause problems in itself. When people are labeled terminal, they may get a different kind of care than other patients. I don't think today we isolate them down in the West Wing like we used to, but it still makes the staff confront their own mortality. I never went for the "you're dying from the minute you're born" theory. I believe you're either alive or you're dead. If you're alive, you should be treated as a valuable human being encouraged to plan, to function, to live.

■ MAKING A BARGAIN

At the bargaining stage, people begin to feel that if they behave, if they're nice, maybe they can postpone the inevitable. If they do everything, like eat the right macrobiotic foods, take the right drugs, and show up for the right treatment they may buy a little more time or beat it altogether. This is a coping mechanism you learn when you're a child and you want something. When things were denied you, you figured that maybe if you were good, emptied the dishwasher every night, and did homework maybe your mother would let you have what you wanted. We're taught that if you're good you get the reward, but if you're angry you won't.

Sometimes bargains are not merely bargaining, but deadline setting, and this is not to be taken lightly. In my work as a hospice nurse, I have seen a lot of people who wanted to live to see their son graduate, or their daughter marry. Once their goal was accomplished, they would often die quickly. Some of the time it may be unrealistic when people say, "I'll live to see you get married," or "Just let me live to see my first grandchild be born," when you know these goals are about five years down the road.

▪ DEPRESSION

Bargaining is usually a short harmless mechanism that may be followed by a depression. When all one's efforts come to naught, the illness can't be denied anymore and there's not enough strength to be angry. It's impossible not to face it anymore. When their job is gone and financial problems set in, and people begin to feel that they are about to lose everyone and everything, they become very sad.

There are two main kinds of depression that you usually see in people dealing with catastrophic illness. In some people it's more of a reactive depression to an immediate cause. For example, a mother who can't parent her child anymore. We had a young woman at the center with AIDS who had two small children. Her sister allowed her to come live with her so she could take care of her, but only under very strict regulations. The sister refused to believe that AIDS was not a communicable disease, no matter how much education we gave her. She wouldn't let this woman touch the refrigerator, wouldn't even let her parent her own children. This young woman suffered an incredible loss. She felt well, and was physically able to parent her children. All she wanted to do was give her child a glass of milk, or change the child's diaper, but her sister would not let her do that. Naturally she was very angry, but she was afraid to express the anger for fear that she would be thrown out with no place to go. Sometimes intervention can help to eliminate a depression that has a specific cause like that.

For the most part, however, people dealing with catastrophic illness enter into a preparatory type of grief over the impending loss. Often people's reaction to someone who is very sad is of course to cheer them up, to be positive, to be bright. The visitor will come in all happy and smiles, and say look at this, look at that, look it's snowing. It's not helpful. The patient needs to be allowed to be very sad. The dying person is in the process of losing everything. It's very hard to deal with them. Not physically hard, but I know as a nurse myself, we're very geared to being doers. If it's pain, give this, do that. It's the same with social workers or other people who are problem solvers. What do you do when there's nothing to do? You can't make this sadness go away. What's happening to them is legitimately very sad. This is when it's hard. There's nothing left to do, and the hardest part is to just be there.

You can't fill out another paper to make this go away, you can't refer them to another agency to help them, but you can't stop going there either. You have to be there for them. This is when all the things that you've learned don't help. What you need to do is just to be there. Hold their hand, listen, or maybe just be quiet and say nothing, but be there.

A lot of times families will say, "Let's cheer them up, we'll have more visitors come." It doesn't help, it hinders. They need to be allowed to go through this emotional preparation. I would encourage you to go visit even though there is nothing to do. That's when they need you most.

■ ACCEPTANCE

The fifth and final coping mechanism is acceptance. When people have been allowed and helped to go through the other stages, they may come to the stage of acceptance. This is a stage that appears to be devoid of overt feelings. They are tired now. They've done their work. They have been allowed to express their denial, their anger, and they've been allowed to mourn their losses. It's certainly not a happy time, but there is no struggle.

A lot of times the family has a hard time with acceptance because it's frustrating. Here is someone who was taking all the treatments, and all of a sudden the struggle is over. The things that they loved to do they may not want to do anymore. They may not want to see the people that they once loved to see. They don't want to watch TV anymore. The family wants to bring a friend in, turn the TV on, thinking it will help. But often, at this point, the social circle gets down to maybe one person. This is a time when they need you. If you are the one who is chosen to be with them when they're dying, it's a very special place to be.

Encourage the mother, the spouse, or the child to be there. There is nothing right or wrong to do. When someone is dying, what difference does the pulse, the blood pressure make? There's nothing to do, but to talk to them, to hold their hand, to treat them like a human being. Even if the person dying hasn't talked for a week, it's better not to talk as if they are not there. They're still very much there and they need you.

People don't go from stage one to stage five in an orderly fashion. It isn't as if you can cheer them on, saying, "Okay, we're on stage two let's move on to three tomorrow, and by next week we'll have this thing wrapped up." Sometimes they may be in denial with you, and anger with someone else. They vary from minute to minute, from month to month, depending on how they feel. A lot of times the family is in one coping mechanism and the patient is in another. You have to support people where they are. Let them be where they are. Let them own it, let them experience it and then they'll move at their own pace.

During all this, they have to have hope. They have to know that you have the compassion to take care of them, that you're going to give them the information that they need, and that there is some hope. They need to know the situation is serious. They need to know, so they can make some plans for what will happen "if." But they also need to know that there is hope for them. This is why I always have a problem with the phrase "terminal illness" because with that comes a sense of hopelessness, which often may come from the staff, or the family. This is when people get tied up into time frames. How much longer does he have?

I had a man call me the other week at the center. His father went home from the hospital with lung cancer. The doctor said he had six months to live. The family geared up for six months. They hired private duty nurses and gave him more care than he had gotten since his wife died and his children moved out of the house. Eight months later the son called to say, "I can't believe it, my father just bought a two-hundred-dollar rowing machine—why? He's already living on borrowed time, how could he?" The man went home, had more care and attention than he'd ever had, and now he had a reason to live. He probably had three meals a day for the first time in ages. Why should he die? But the family had geared up for the six months, and they were knocked off balance. They didn't know what to do.

When I was a hospice nurse, I once predicted that a patient had about two days to live. The family flew in from California, and I don't need to tell you what happened. Everybody wanted to be there for the death, the funeral, and get it all in on one round-trip ticket. Needless to say, this man lived on and I will never predict another death as long as I live.

One last thing that really helps is a sense of humor. Don't think because you're dealing with people who are terminally ill, that laughter isn't welcome. Since I've been working at the center, I've seen people who deal with incredible amounts of different losses, people who are catastrophically ill, and they often laugh. When people are alive, no matter what, they can still laugh, they can still love. They are first and foremost human beings, a condition that ties us all together, and what I think we owe each other most of all is respect.

3

THE HEARING HEART

By Mary Ann Collins, R.N., M.A.

MARY ANN COLLINS *has her master of arts in psychiatric nursing with a clinical specialty in grief, loss, bereavement and catastrophic illness. She is the director of the Hackensack Hospice Program in Bergen County, New Jersey.*

I think one of the most important things you can learn when you're dealing with people, from a professional perspective in any helping way, especially when you're dealing with a whole family crisis and certainly death is crisis, is to be a good listener and to do what we've been taught to do in nursing. And that is to assess the situation. And the only way to assess the situation and to find out what the needs of the family are, is to see what's going on, watch the dynamics and be able to pick up on the strengths and weaknesses in each individual, and how you as a professional can intervene and bring out the strengths.

You interact with the family in a compassionate, sharing type of way, but in your head you're leading the family in some ways to give you data that is eventually going to help you guide them. You're using those professional skills, but you're not coming in with a notebook and asking questions. Sometimes it looks like you're being social. Yet, you learn quite a lot in your informal interview. Before I go in, I ask myself, What is it I need to know about this family today? I plan it so that by the time I leave, I've given them information to work with some of the critical issues.

You need to discover, for instance, what the family process was like prior to the illness. A lot of times you can do that by going right to the primary caregiver. Say the caregiver is the wife and the person who is dying is the husband. Suppose there's three or four children. You may say to the wife, "Before your husband got ill, what was it like here? What was your role as the parent in the house?" You may find out that she worked, that she was responsible for the bills. You look at a person like that and you say to yourself, this isn't going to be so difficult for her because the only thing that has changed here is that now they have a sick person to care for and that sick person isn't adding to the income, so what does that mean? Does it mean that the primary care person is now still out working? If that person is still out working, then it tells you there is a need here. During the period of time that the person is out working someone has to be here to care for the person who's ill. If the wife has to work, what's going to happen when the patient needs to be medicated? By getting some of those answers, you are already being filled in on either the strengths or the weaknesses.

A lot of times while you're talking with someone, you're watching for special behavior. Is she clinging? Is she pining? Whiny? In your head you have to start to say, this person is going to have major difficulty when their loved one dies because they're not letting go. For example, the wife may say to you, "I didn't even drive, he drove me every place."

One of the ways you can help is by saying to the care person, "Have you thought about what's going to happen now when he does die? How are you going to be able to get around?" Then the person can talk about that and get in touch with it and maybe even at that point recognize what they may need to do for themselves. You're never going to be able to tell them how to handle it because it's their situation. It's very important that anybody who goes in as a professional, from the beginning recognizes that this is the family's turf. You're not going in there to tell them what to do. You're not going in there to rearrange their lives, you're going in to help them. My role is to help them problem solve around a situation that they are not ready to deal with in many instances.

For example, when a forty-year-old man is dying it might mean the wife now has to become the total breadwinner, both parents to the children, be a primary care person, function as a home health aide—so many things, it's just overwhelming. And that's what you have to look for. In most instances people can gather strength if they feel support and they trust you—that's very, very, important. I establish trust by not being too high-pressure. I usually go in and allow them to talk about the painful situation and I communicate my concern for them. I validate that what they're going through at this particular point in time is terrible, and the fact that they feel out of control is understandable. Many times they may be angry and act angry with me. One of the ways I deal with this is I never argue with the person. I try to defuse it by saying, "You know, you're right. At a time like this, it must be difficult for you."

I had a woman on the phone last week who was really angry. What had happened was that she had sent a donation to our hospice in memory of her nephew and my secretary had overlooked a note that came with the donation. She wanted the acknowledgement to go to Aunt so-and-so and the children, but the secretary just took the name off the top of the check, which was Mr. and Mrs. so-and-so, and it just so happened that this woman's husband was dead. The more she talked, the angrier she got and I realized that she had not resolved the issues surrounding the death of her husband. So I listened to her and I said, "I apologize." She said, "And that letter was signed by you." I said, "You're right. It was signed by me, and it was not meant in any way to cause you any more discomfort and pain than you must be going through right now, having lost your nephew. Please accept my apology." So I gave her control and let her give me direction as to how she wanted it handled. Then I sat down and hand-wrote a letter to her nephew's widow explaining the mix-up. Then I wrote a letter to the woman herself reiterating how sorry I was and that certainly at a time like this she did not need this added stress.

I saw it. I saw a woman who was screaming in rage just mellow out by the end of the conversation because I said that I had made a mistake. Regardless of the fact that she was still in her own grief, these were her feelings and she was angry and she needed to feel that she had some control to change things. She needed me to be contrite about it, which is exactly what I gave her. In many instances, it isn't helpful to try to clarify situations for the person or try to turn it around because they don't want to be wrong.

When I am on a case, I try to be there for the whole family, not just for the patient. When you have someone who's dying, if you don't try to maintain equilibrium for the entire family system, you're not going to be able to do anything for the patient. Whether it's birth or death, you're still dealing with a family. If that family has been maladapted for a few years, you're not going to change that. You can deal with keeping this maladapted family intact throughout the process of the patient's dying, so the patient can be maintained as comfortably as possible.

The primary care person is also going through a process of their own—a death process. They're losing that person in their life. Whether they've been madly in love with that person or not, that person has been an intricate part of their life and they've chosen and elected to care for that person, therefore they must be validated. They need to be cared for and you can do that for them. If they say, "Last night I was furious at him, I keep thinking to myself, he's not fighting," then I say, "I understand what you're going through. It must be very difficult to have someone that you love dying." Sometimes what they really need is to cry and say, "I want him to live, I don't want him to die."

If they ask me unanswerable questions like, "Why is God doing this to me?" I'm honest with them. I tell them that I have no answers in that realm. That's why I believe that you need an interdisciplinary approach, because at that point I ask them if they would like to meet with the chaplain. Because you can't ignore it, you can't ignore the fact that they're in the spiritual domain. But I tell them honestly, that the only thing I can do is tell them how I feel from my perspective. I say, "I'm not living with what you're living with at this point in time, and it sounds to me like that's an important question for you. I can make a suggestion. Would you like the chaplain? Have you contacted your local priest, rabbi or minister? They may not have the answers as to what God has in mind, but they may be able to direct you or give you insight. I have no answers." So I listen and I ask, "Would it be helpful to you to have the chaplain get in touch with you? It sounds to me like you have some spiritual questions." What I'm doing is acknowledging that I may not be able to answer their questions, but I'm not ignoring their need.

My primary purpose is to help the whole family unit. Sometimes the patient may be saying one thing, the wife saying something else, and the children are saying something else. If that's the case, I may say, "It seems to me that all of you have some unanswered questions or issues that you need to deal with and you're speaking to me about them. I'm more than comfortable to listen, and support you. I understand that you're having pain and concern about it, but it's been my experience that the only way you can rectify it and get some answers is to talk about it among yourselves. I would be happy to be there as a facilitator if you would like."

I was working with an AIDS patient once who was running back and forth to the doctor all the time. It was my understanding that he had this gusto to live, and in the beginning he certainly did. Somewhere along the line I lost track of the fact that he didn't really want to continue to fight this way. Not that he didn't want to live, but he was tired of fighting for his life. He wanted to relax and rest a little, but he felt pressured by his mother. It was his mother's need to run him back and forth to doctors, and to put him on interferon and all these things, that was making him uncomfortable and didn't seem to be doing anything for him. That's what he told me and I said to him, "Have you said that to your mother?" He said he didn't think he could do that. I asked him why and he said, "Because I might let her down." I asked him if it would be helpful if we all met so the two of them could talk openly about what was going on. I told him that I had a feeling, when I talked to his mother, that she was doing all of this for him because she thought that was what he wanted. He agreed and realized that was exactly what was going on.

She was running all over the place and it was destroying her because nothing was working and neither of them communicated about it. As the nurse, you're getting information from this person and you're getting information from that person. Obviously, without breaking confidentiality, you are able to piece things together. But until you get them together to open up and talk about what's going on, there's nothing that can be done about it. You can't resolve these issues for them, so the only thing you can say is, "I have the feeling that this is the way you feel."

So I talked to this man's mother. I told her I could see how upset she was because nothing was working for him. And I asked her why she kept pushing him. She told me she couldn't let him down because he wanted to go for it. Then I said, "What if he didn't want to go for it?" She looked at me and I said, "You know, I'm getting the feeling that he doesn't and I'm wondering if the two of you would like to talk about it." They did, and they cried because what they were agreeing upon was that they had nothing to work on. Even though there is no proven cure for AIDS, somehow the idea of working on it gives you that little ray of hope.

Someone once said to me that what made her so sad, particularly with all the new age talk about being responsible for your own disease, was that before her son died he said he felt like a failure because he had said before that he wasn't going to die, and now he was dying. To combat this type of thinking I have my patients take a look at what they've done and try to make them realize that they've done everything within their control and capabilities, and if it didn't work that doesn't make them a failure. They've tried the system. The system has failed them because there is nothing built into the system that can change what has happened to them.

There seems to be some kind of guilt attached to dying. People who get into that are spiritual people, really. I haven't dealt with any atheists who evaluate themselves in terms of bad, good or indifferent. They don't even use those words. People who get into that kind of thing are definitely spiritual people. I tell them I can't help them with it and that I can only deal with my own spirituality, and I'm not so sure about that all the time. I usually refer them to our chaplain, Sister Pat, and she really helps people to look at the loving God.

I can understand people going to every extreme with diets and running here and there, as long as the hope is realistic. If someone says to me on their death bed that three years from now they're going to be in Germany, that's unrealistic. I would have to say, "How do you think you're going to accomplish that? You're rather sick right now, how do you think you're going to do that?" I'd have to work with them on that. I have helped people get to a point where they don't believe they're going to be in Germany in three years.

One of the people that I worked with knew he was going to die, but he wanted to fight. He has now abandoned the therapies and diet, but I did encourage him to try for awhile. We talked about it, and he tried and then he went through a struggle, too, having to abandon the methods. But even today he still talks of the possibility of a cure, and that's okay because who am I to say no? He talks about a cure although he knows that would be a miracle. He's depressed.

It's hard to know what to do with depression. Mostly it's a word that I don't use. I've been told not to use it. I have a client who told me, "Mary Ann, I hate that word," and I said, "Okay, we won't use it." And I won't use it when it's inappropriate. It's appropriate to be depressed sometimes. If you know you're dying it's inappropriate to be off in la-la land, planning trips or parties. If I saw that going on, I'd be more concerned than if someone is saying to me, "I'm depressed."

If a patient brings it up, I will say, "Tell me about your depression. What are the kinds of things you think about that make you feel depressed?" Let them air it. Most people don't hang on to that depression forever. People don't like feeling depressed so they try to shake it on their own if they can. One way is by trying to get up out of bed. It gives them some meaning to their lives. Another way is by focusing in on some of the good things in their life. Meditation, relaxation, good music, humor, reading a funny book, listening to a funny tape—those kinds of things help. And sometimes when all else fails, I talk to their physician about putting them on an antidepressant if it gets real bad.

What's difficult is when I dislike a patient, or have some real problems with a patient. It happened to me once with a woman who was a social worker, who had to maintain the control, who was not nice. I had to be honest and look at it and say, I cannot be therapeutic with her. I was too angry at her, so I gave her to somebody else. I don't necessarily have to like somebody to be therapeutic with them, but it got too difficult and I thought, I'm not doing her any good and that's not fair to her. The other person did very well with her.

Losing control can be a big issue for the patient. I try to hone in on the things that they feel out of control about.

Obviously it's the disease, but they usually don't identify it. They'll identify things in the house that annoy them. Meals are usually served and they're not asked for their input, so we look at those practical things. The primary care person is brought in and we talk about the patient and how he would really like his meals. In a sense I am an interpreter, facilitating communication between patient and caregiver without causing hurt feelings or turmoil. I have to establish a rapport with that family so they can trust me.

Sometimes it gets to be a situation where each one wants me for their special ally. I try to pick up on that and give each person a lot of positive feedback before I ever try to change the system. In other words, I tell them how well they are doing things and begin to make them feel like I'm looking at them in a very positive way. Then when I make suggestions or make a change, I might tell them about a family I worked with in the past that had a similar problem. For instance, they might be having trouble giving medication. I'll say to the primary care person, when the patient is having trouble swallowing, "You're the one who knows him the best, what do you think he likes?" Then I'll suggest they give the medication in that, say applesauce, for example.

Another important thing is to help the primary care person not feel responsible for it, if the patient is refusing to eat. You get them in touch with the fact that when someone is dying, it's a normal process to withdraw from food. Then they can be free to not be in there every fifteen minutes trying to feed them.

Education is a very big component. We have the knowledge. The families are scared; they didn't go to nursing school. This is the first person they're dealing with who's dying. So sit down and educate them, tell them everything.

In most instances, when the doctor refers to hospice, they pretty much leave it in our hands. It's difficult for the doctors many times to give the ominous news. For example, the other day a patient was being referred and the person talking on the phone to the family member said, "We'll teach you what to do. Your mother's cancer has metastasized to the liver." And the caller said, "To the liver!" Our nurse said, "I'm sorry I had to be the one to tell you, but you need to know it because if you start to see your mom acting confused and turning yellow, you need to know that." It's not fair when you've given somebody the job of taking care of someone to keep any information from them. If a doctor wants to withhold information, I have to say, "I'm sorry, we can't do that."

I had a doctor tell us that he didn't want us to tell the family that we're hospice. He told us to say we were from the visiting nurse service. We cannot work with someone under those conditions. Because if they find out (and there's hospice written all over our brochures), if we put a volunteer in and they mention hospice, this person will not trust us. If they don't trust us, how can we work with them? So this physician said, "Okay, tell them."

One of the things we do before we take a case on is try to get the primary care person into the office so we can evaluate what's going on with them. We do this before we go into their home, to let them deal with some of the feelings before the nurse arrives on the scene. That allows them to focus on their feelings.

All the listening, interpreting, education, and helping to express, can be a tremendous support. Support means they can call me. They can get us twenty-four hours a day if they need us. Even if they don't think it's important but their heart is scared, they can pick up the phone and we'll be there. We answer their questions gently and put our arms around them. We tell them what a wonderful job they're doing. We remind them that it's easy for us to come in for a couple of hours, but that what they're doing, being there almost constantly, is difficult and demanding. We acknowledge who they are and that they are doing something very special and important. And that if they feel angry about it at times, that's okay.

There might be a situation where the wife is the primary caregiver and she's supported by family members who are in denial. Maybe her parents won't talk about her husband's approaching death. Then what we need to do is just talk to the primary care person about her feelings and then evaluate whether or not these parents, with a facilitator, will reckon with the reality. Sometimes they can't. In that case you have to look for somebody else in the family environment that can provide her with the support that the parents can't give. Maybe a close friend or sibling. So you help them to look around for the options.

I run into people whose parents can't deal with it or whose friends can't deal with it, who feel abandoned. What can we do about that? First of all we take a look at their feelings and we validate them. I would feel the same way. It must be difficult.

I'm seeing a woman now in counseling whose best friend was there for her through the death of her husband and who now has abandoned her. This woman has called and has reached out, and this friend cannot even call her back. What does she feel about it? She has a lot of anger. I help her express it and ask her if there's anything else she feels she needs to do with it. One of the things she wanted to do was to sit down and write a letter to this person about how sorry she feels over the loss of that friendship on top of the loss of her husband, explaining that she has extended herself to the best of her ability and now she has to let go. And that's what she did. She wrote and said, "If you can't respond to me, I can't pursue you anymore." If I were her, I would be angry too.

With hospice, we can help people maintain a normal household when it's not a normal household. We have someone who does wonderful work with kids, helping them to express feelings, working with art therapy and bringing them together with other kids who are going through similar things.

It's up to us, when we go in, to evaluate how the kids are coping. In most instances, the parents are very worried about the kids. They are really concerned about their children because they recognize that most of their energy is going to the person who is dying. What we do is sit down and talk about what they can do to help the kids process a little bit of the situation, and what their feelings are. By process, I mean analyze, speak out, actively participate. We help the parent to relax and not try to hide anything from the children because children learn to grieve as they see their parents grieve. If they see their parents holding in the tears they're going to do the same thing. I encourage the parents to express their feelings. Talk to the children about how they feel and accept them where they are.

Children will never feel what a couple feels about each other. The parents have to recognize that those kids aren't going to go months and years feeling what the adults feel. If the child won't come in and talk to the one who's sick, I try to make time to talk to the kids and ask them how they're doing. I try to get them to open up.

It's been my experience that the family sees me as a helpful support system through this crisis and someone they can count on.

I have even maintained friendships with families long after the person has died. Getting close to people before they die takes its toll and there are times when I'm over-whelmed with sadness. I let it out. I cry. I get in touch with it, but not in front of the patient. I will show tears when there's sadness, but I don't fall apart with the family.

I remember one case I had with a woman who I grew to love so much. She was just a beautiful person. My last visit was on a Friday and she was expected to die within twenty-four hours. I rode home and just cried and cried. I went to the wake and sat with the family for awhile. This was a few years ago and it still brings tears to my eyes. I still think of her with a great deal of love. She was a beautiful person who taught me a lot about dignity. She was a dignified lady who accepted death. She was very spiritual and she accepted that this was the end of her life. She made sense out of her life and there was some sadness. One of her daughters was really emotionally disturbed, and she wept about that, that she couldn't change it and that it was sad for this daughter. Open, honest, accepting, she loved God, loved people, and she was grateful. She'd say thank you for everything and was really peaceful with her death.

Working with people who are dying has taught me a lot about living. I don't know when my time to die will be. I don't know what I'm going to be like when I do find out I'm going to die. For all I know it could happen suddenly. But I'm not terrified of it anymore. I believe that it is just a stepping stone and that I'm going to be okay. There is no way to exempt yourself. If I were to be told tomorrow that I had a terminal illness and there was nothing that could be done, I would weep because I love my family and I love what I have, but I have no regrets either. That's the gift I received, doing what I'm doing. By working in the area of death, I have been given the gift of getting in touch with life on a daily basis, making sure I enjoy and get the most out of it, the fullness out of it.

I just think of all the people that have invited me in at one of the most vulnerable and significant times of their lives. It really does bring you in intimate contact with people rather than superficial relationships. I never have superficial relationships with anyone anymore. If I start a relationship now, I climb right in and the fact is I know you can get hurt in a relationship, but I wouldn't sacrifice that for anything because the other part of it is, if you don't climb in then you cheat yourself out of the possibility of enhancing your life.

There aren't any rules in working with death and dying. I learned that people who are dying are so honest.

I remember a woman who was dying with her arms open and I knew she was in touch with God. There are so many things that I've seen. What that has done for me is to verify that this isn't it, this isn't all there is. I've gained so very much. And I used to be cancer-phobic and death-phobic. Petrified. When I was younger, I was running to doctors constantly, thinking I was going to die and that cancer was going to get me, and I realized I could either do this for the rest of my life or I could say, "Wait a minute, let's get in touch with what's going on here and find out what this is all about. What am I afraid of here?" And hopefully, I'd snap out of it without anticipating every day of my life that I was going to die. That's really what happened for me. In a way, that led me deeper into death and dying. I needed to do something.

Both of my parents died around the same time, within six months of each other, and I got very involved in caring for them. I remember kneeling in church one day, and I said to God, "How can I improve the quality of my life here on Earth and my family's life? I don't know what you want of me; take me wherever it's going to take me, but let me be of help and service." I really wanted to be of service. I let go that day. I didn't decide my destiny. Before that, my plans were to go to nursing school, to finish getting a masters and teach. That has all changed, because essentially I do hands-on service with patients. I think that has released me.

4

AUTHENTICITY AND FLEXIBILITY

By Father Charlie Hudson
The Center for Hope Hospice

F ATHER CHARLIE HUDSON *is a Roman Catholic priest who has spent most of his ministry in hospitals where he began to specialize in work with the terminally ill. Finding that the bureaucracy and financial demands of the hospital setting were not conducive to care of terminal patients, Father Hudson developed a non-profit, non-sectarian hospice program.*

The purpose of our home-care program is to enhance the quality of life for patients who are considered to be terminally ill with a life expectancy of three to six months. Our aim is to remove distressing physical, emotional and psychological symptoms. We try to help people deal with those symptoms and to free themselves to be able to enjoy life to the fullest at home, surrounded by loved ones.

From a personal viewpoint, I think what brought me into this field was the fact that both my parents died of terminal illnesses at the young ages of forty-two and fifty-six, and my two younger brothers died in tragic accidents at twelve and twenty-one, making me the last survivor in my family. I think once you've walked through that dark valley yourself and experienced the anger, hurt, frustration and bitterness—and you resolve some of it and move on—you become more human. You either become very bitter, hard and withdraw completely from humanity or you deepen and become much more sensitive and caring toward other people who are experiencing the same things you have experienced.

We resolve our feelings with the support of other people. People who are willing to listen. People who are willing to accept our feelings and emotions no matter what they might be, and as absurd and bizarre as they might be.

The ongoing deep faith that I have in terms of my own religious tradition has been strengthened through my work in the field of death and dying. I continue to believe that life is transition, and that others who have gone before us are still with us. As Thornton Wilder said, "There is a land of the living and a land of the dead and the bridge is love." That bond is still there. I don't see death as a final separation. While it's painful, I believe that I will see the people who have gone before me again.

The ability to get out my emotions in the presence of others has helped me to heal. That and my faith have enabled me to survive and to move on to where I am now—involving myself in the lives of other people who are experiencing what I did. They do get through it without religion. Religious experience is part of spirituality, but the spirituality can be present in a person's life without any religious expression. So many people come to us who have deep spiritual bonds between themselves and those they are leaving behind.

When a person is dying, they need to be assured of the fact that they've been loved. They want to have an integration of their life. They want to be able to pull all of their experiences together to see that they've had meaning and value, that somehow their life has made a difference to somebody. They do this usually through dialogue with significant people in their lives. They need to have their life affirmed as they tell their life story, whether it be to a member of their family or to a member of my staff, and to have them understand that they had good moments.

Once you get people talking, it flows. You just have to ask some basic questions like, "What has life been for you? Have you ever felt yourself in a situation similar to where you are now? What was your family like? What was it like growing up in your family? How did your family handle crises? What are some moments in your life that you really feel proud of?" They want to look back on something and say, "This is what I accomplished."

Caregivers can be good listeners because of the bond of trust between them and the dying person. People relate to each other not only because of the things they say to, or do for, one another, but because of what they become to each other. And the becoming process is the mystery. Why does someone decide to allow you to become their friend? You might want to become their friend, but they might not allow that to happen. But if the chemistry is right, the person says, "You know, there's something about you I like. I feel safe with you." So they choose you to be their friend and they tell you things they wouldn't tell everybody. At the core of every human being there's an essential need to leave behind something in another human being so that when they are gone this other person continues the legacy.

One of the most spiritual moments I had with somebody involved a buzz saw. I was visiting John who had built an addition on to his house, and shortly after that he became quite sick and was dying. One day while we were talking, we heard a buzz saw outside, someone was cutting down trees. It was so loud that it was distracting to me and I said to him, "John, doesn't that bother you?" But he said, "I love that sound because I'm a carpenter by trade, and when I hear it, it reminds me of all the things I was able to do." Now, even though he's gone, any time I hear a buzz saw John comes into focus.

A similar thing occurs with songs and places. They're connecting points between us and those who have gone before. I think that's very, very important. If I were dying and I was leaving anyone behind, I would like to think that every time they heard a certain song, or experienced whatever it was that we shared together, they would remember me. That's the human part of us that wants to remain eternal.

As a priest, people sometimes look to me for answers. If someone begins to ask me direct questions like, "Why is this happening?" or, "Why is God doing this to me?" I usually say that I'm not God's defense attorney and I can't explain what's happening. But I know one thing. What's happening to them now is going to happen to me. I know it. In some way, in some form, it will happen because very few of us get out of life without some measure of suffering.

I have said, "Why is this happening to you now? I don't know. Except I know, because of my faith in God, that He has sent me at this time into your life to be with you, to make whatever you have to endure a little bit more bearable because you don't have to do it alone." I think that's the only promise that God has ever given us, that He would not let us be alone. Therefore, it is our responsibility as human beings who have a faith in God, to realize that we channel God's love and compassion to one another. If I don't believe that, religion doesn't mean anything to me.

There are people who embrace religion who would not even think about serving at someone else's bedside. A lot of my volunteers believe that this is a mission, that this is something that God has called them to do. They come from many different religious backgrounds.

When I was a young priest and going through a nursing home, on the wall it said very bluntly, "Where you are now I once was, and where I am now you will one day be." And if you ever forget that, then you're only kidding yourself. What right do we have, when our turn comes, to expect others to give us what we failed to give to others? So many times I've seen people all alone because their life was lived specifically for themselves. They fitted people into their life when it was convenient for them. They gave when they would benefit from the giving and held back when there was no profit in the giving. I've seen other people who have given everything that they had, literally down to their last piece of clothing, and I've seen the difference in the two dying. Those who have given die in peace because they aren't holding on to anything.

When someone is afraid, we try to walk with them as far as we can. We want to be there for them when they need us, but not intrude when they don't need us. In all the people I've seen die, there is a moment that comes where they make a decision to let go and stop the struggle against what's happening and they go with the flow. Being who we are as human beings, we want to be in control. We always want to be calling the shots and be on top of things. It's no different when we die, it's still the struggle. Usually what happens in ninety percent of the cases is that the person gets to the point where they say, "I'm going to let go, I'm not going to fight and struggle." If the family can then give them permission to let go, it's a lot more peaceful. When the family is still struggling and wants to fight, and the patient wants to let go, it's very hard.

Rarely have I seen anyone die that hasn't reached that point of acceptance. And it's not unlike anything else in life. For instance, if someone walks out of your life, you fight against it and struggle and finally you make a decision that it's not going to change, so now you have to change. You have to somehow accept it, let it go and move on. *When* that happens, I don't know. Being human and being imperfect, it's important to struggle and it's important to fight for what we can change, but it's also important to know when we cannot change what's happening. We can find a new approach to what's happening and feel some serenity and peace in that. Struggle is part of the human process and I don't think it will ever not be there. You reach the ultimate moment when you say, I am powerless and I can't change what may be happening in this situation so I'll make the only decision that I can make, which is to accept it. And I'll do the best I can with it.

I see it in the dying and I see it in the living. I've maintained that death isn't something that happens at the end of a person's life. Death is something that happens every time there is a significant ending in a person's life, and they have to let go and say goodbye to all that has been before they move on to what will be.

Too many times people deny their humanness because they don't express their hurt and their pain, and as a result, they're only living half of a life. They're rushing on to what's coming. I see it in weddings. The father walks his daughter down the aisle and when they reach the altar he has to let go of her hand and give it to someone else. Someone else is going to step in then and become to her what he had been up to that point. Many fathers cry at weddings because underneath they know that while it's a joyful occasion, something is ending. Usually, there is much talk about the wedding but not about the loss.

Working with the dying has sensitized me to the value of today. I know there is an old cliche, "live every day to the fullest." It's valuable advice, but nobody ever heeds it. I think that when you work with the dying, they give you life. They give you a new perspective, a new value for life. You no longer take it for granted. I look at this fifty-three-year-old man who's dying and I think, that could be me because I'm fifty-three years old. Then I remember that if this person is leaving and I'm still here, it is for a purpose and I had better find out what that purpose is and fulfill it. Otherwise my life's going to be empty.

The experience of working with terminally ill patients has helped fulfill me and my staff. I've seen joy in my work. I remember on Mother's Day, we had a patient by the name of Janet. She was a fifty-one-year-old nurse. She was dying and knew it, and she was ready. She was Catholic, so we had a Mass in the room. There was a lot of joy in that room. You see, joy is different than happiness. Happiness is more of a surface thing. One poet said, "The more you pursue happiness, the more it eludes you." It's like the butterfly. If you just stand still, sometimes the butterfly will land on your shoulder. Joy is something that resides more deeply in the spirit of an individual, so that even in the midst of anxiety, suffering and pain, a person can have a sense of joy.

When my mother was dying, even though it was painful, there was a sense of joy because we were able to share on a deep level. It's that kind of joy that continues even after death. You come away with a sense of sadness and you cry, but there's also a part of you that feels joy because you took care of what needed to be taken care of. Would you say you were happy? No. Would you say you were joyful? Yes. I think the joy goes into the spirit of the person. I saw it in Janet. I saw it in her eyes and in her face. There was a serenity, a peace there. There was a joy that I've seen in some patients. Not all. Some patients struggle and scream and holler right to the end. Many of our patients deny what's happening because it's their only way of coping. But they're allowed to do this. They die their own way. Exactly the way they lived in many instances. Whatever existed in that family while they were alive is probably going to be there up to the moment of death. If the family did not relate on a deep level during life, they're probably not going to start doing it when the person is dying.

One thing that really adds to the hospice environment is humor. I found that patients, even in pain, can laugh. Once, I was called to a patient's house. Peggy was dying and she seemed to really be in a lot of pain. I went in to administer the sacraments of the church, and as I was praying with her, she was moving in the bed. I thought, "My God, she's in so much pain." I began hurrying the prayers and rushing through the ritual. When it was all over I said, "Peggy, I'm sorry it took so long, you're in so much pain." She said, "Father, I'm not in pain, I'm on the bedpan." We both laughed so hard her son came in to see what we were laughing about. We told him and he started to laugh.

Another time, I was with an Italian fellow who had been married to a tough matriarch. She ran that whole family. When Mama spoke, everybody jumped. This poor guy probably never spoke two words in his whole life, especially in the presence of his wife. Her funeral was on a hot day in July. At the cemetery as Mama was getting buried, Papa comes up and stands next to me. At that exact moment a tremendous thunder storm came up. Fortunately, there was a tent. He leaned over and said, "I guess she arrived." And I said, "What?" and he said, "I guess she arrived!" And then his two daughters came up and asked what we were laughing at, and I said, "Papa said your Mama just got in." And they laughed.

There's a lot of laughter here among our staff. We have a patient now that lives in a rat-infested place in the city, and he hadn't had a bath in about six weeks. He had no clothes, and he was dying, but ambulatory. We took him over to our place and gave him a bath and he didn't want to come out of the tub. He was in there for over two hours. The secretary kept waiting. She wanted to close up and our driver was waiting, so finally we got him some clothes and shoes and took him home. The next day, when our nurse went to take him for treatment, he was so excited about the shoes and coat that he turned on some music and the two of them began dancing. He had his little hat tipped in front and he danced all the way down to the treatment center. He was so happy.

Now, here's this man who's dying, who's got nothing, who lives in a rat-infested place, and has no shoes or clothes to wear. Yet, there was a lot happiness in him because the nurse danced with him. It's like the sun coming out from behind the clouds for a while. Everything looks dark, and all of a sudden the sun breaks through and you think, Hey, it's going to be a nice day. Even if the storm is still going to come, you're catching a few rays. That's what it's like with the dying. You know eventually it's going to end and they're going through a period of distress, but if you can bring some moments into their lives in which they feel touched and loved, then it's mutual. You come away enriched. If you asked my nurses what it's like working with the dying, they would say, "We've gotten more than we've given."

I think the thing that makes our hospice program different is that we built a team first. A lot of hospices start by rushing out to see the patients before the team gets to know each other. It's important to build a support system within the team. We took weekend retreats together and built our team, and then we went out to work with patients. If one of our nurses comes back to the office when someone is dying, there is always someone to talk to. We have a tightly knit support group. Most of our nurses go to the wakes and funerals, and it brings some closure in their relationship with the patient. We have a very low burnout rate.

If I have any advice for a new caregiver, it is to be authentic. In other words, be yourself, be flexible and be able to be present without needing to talk. If I don't see authenticity and flexibility in a person, they can't work with us because I don't want somebody being something that they're not, and I don't want somebody who can't adapt themselves to what another person believes about life. We're not in the conversion business. We're not trying to get people to be where we want them to be. We want them to be where they are. If you're at peace with yourself and know what you believe, you don't need to sell it, or convert anybody. I've related to people of all religions and people with no religion. Some of my most memorable moments with patients have transcended religious belief.

The point is that we're here together. We're here together and what is it that we need to be for each other?

You tell me what you need me to be for you. Your confidant, your confessor, your friend or what? Tell me what you need. Do you need an intermediary between you and your family? I will try to be that for you.

As caregivers, we need to be true to ourselves and at the same time, be flexible for the patient. But most of all, we need to be there.

5
SELF-HONESTY

By Bob Sproul
AIDS Case Manager

BOB SPROUL *is on staff at The Center for Help in Time of Loss. He is a certified HIV-antibody testing counselor who connects HIV-infected individuals to the resources and services they need, and establishes resources where none exist. A founding member of New Jersey Buddies and Coalition on AIDS, Sproul is also an experienced facilitator of support groups and President of the North Jersey AIDS Alliance. He provides AIDS education to the community, health care volunteers and professionals.*

Over the years, all of us tend to develop some subtle and perhaps not-so-subtle prejudices. In our role as caregivers, the mind-set we bring with us has special significance since it may be the first human input that a patient receives at a most vulnerable and suggestible time. Serious illness often brings with it a feeling of powerlessness, self-doubt and a vague sense of guilt for having caused the problem. If the caregiver's attitude blocks compassionate interaction, the patient's low self-esteem is validated and reinforced, and the commitment to a healing relationship may well be subverted.

Medical epidemics have, historically, been catalysts for the surfacing of many of our deepest anxieties, from fear of the unknown to fear and denial of our own mortality. Those afflicted by cholera, typhoid, influenza, polio and cancer have usually experienced some degree of stigmatization, anger, and abandonment by their societies. AIDS patients experience this type of stigma constantly. And it is compounded by the fact that many "victims" of AIDS are homosexuals and drug addicts—two groups that society already tends to discriminate against. Homophobia (the irrational fear of, or hatred for, homosexuals) in many cases affects the quality of care that AIDS patients receive. In this chapter, I will address the question of whether the caregiver can bring empathy, open mindedness and compassion to a patient who is a member of a group which the caregiver has learned to regard as inferior or immoral.

Lanny was a gay man who was tested for an AIDS-related opportunistic illness. His positive diagnosis for AIDS was reported to him by his family doctor as follows: "Well, with the lifestyle you've led, I don't have to tell you, you've got it."

Given the societal messages that Lanny had received all his life about his "perverted lifestyle" and the current fundamentalist pronouncements that "the wages of homosexuality is AIDS," Lanny was at a crucially vulnerable point. The glib, homophobic message from his doctor reinforced all of the guilt he had been fighting and, conceivably, made him less likely to engage in an energetic, positive program of treatment for his condition.

In addition to the emotional damage done by prejudice, there are physical-health ramifications which often manifest as a result of a caregiver's negative mind-set. If a health aide thinks that drug addicts or homosexuals are "low-lifes" and have brought their conditions on themselves, this may result in less comprehensive and committed care. Bathrooms are often not properly cleaned and housekeeping duties around the bed are neglected, leading to obvious hygiene compromises. Food may be left outside the AIDS patient's door resulting in a cold and unappealing meal, to say nothing of the effect of such overt discrimination on the patient's appetite.

Lack of proper education about disease transmission can lead to other problems which can be extremely demoralizing to the afflicted person, such as the wearing of masks or gloves when it is not appropriate and the avoidance of physical contact with a patient who is often isolated and in need of human touch.

The culture we are raised in teaches us value systems that, unfortunately, include discrimination based on race, sex, sexual orientation and class. Caregivers must be willing to look inside themselves non-judgmentally and identify those areas of prejudice which could block proper and compassionate interaction with a patient.

Being a member of a stigmatized group does not always preclude one's being prejudiced against members of that group. The gay man who is raised in a homophobic environment is likely to internalize the majority point of view and become judgmental toward other gays, as long as he has not integrated his own sexual orientation into a healthy, comfortable self-image. As a "heterosexualized" gay man, I bought the mind-set that being gay is only acceptable in the context of a monogamous relationship, and that promiscuous behavior is immature, self-indulgent and unhealthy. I carried this holier-than-thou point of view into my first experience as a buddy to a young man with AIDS.

Rick was in his late twenties and was acutely ill with several opportunistic illnesses when I first met him. He was very open and was quick to recount his hundreds upon hundreds of sexual adventures. While he did not hide the fact that he had been enthusiastically involved in the sexual fast lane, he did feel that AIDS was a direct consequence of those experiences and that he had betrayed God's plan in some way. It did not surprise me that he had such feelings given the Fundamentalist Christian messages that the media is constantly alluding to, and his own strongly dogmatic religious upbringing. What did surprise and disturb me was that on a very deep level, I agreed with him.

My saving grace in the situation was my involvement in support groups which allowed me to examine my feelings. In addressing and acknowledging my own mind-set, I was able to begin moving through it. I was able to see several things which contributed to my narrow view of Rick's sexual activity.

Firstly, I was strongly influenced by the pervasive view of my generation, my role models, and my religion that heterosexual, monogamous marriage is the only appropriate vehicle in which to express sexual desire. The fact that I no longer believed those messages intellectually, in no way erased the very deep effect my early programming had on me.

Secondly, I was jealous and jealousy was hard for me to accept in myself. This young man had come to sexual awareness during the "free love" era and was open enough to seek out experiences which, to some degree, I felt I had missed out on.

Lastly, I had the imprint of a lifetime of admonitions against practicing what the Bible seemingly said was contrary to the will of Almighty God. Again, the fact that my adult education told me a loving God is not concerned with how individuals express affection for each other, was not enough to completely erase messages impressed upon me at an early age.

The groups I was in allowed me to view these mindsets in a supportive, non-judgmental atmosphere. I was then able to recognize my feelings when I was with Rick and keep them from blocking the trust we needed to bring quality to Rick's life.

As a postscript to my experience with Rick, I might add that several years later I still believe in a committed, monogamous relationship for myself because it seems to fit me well. But I have gotten to a point where I can more easily accept the fact that feeling a particular way for myself does not mean that I have to feel threatened by, or judgmental of, someone who embraces a different philosophy. Indeed, I can enjoy and learn from others' differences.

While some caregivers seemingly operate on such a high spiritual consciousness that they arrive at each new situation with the same degree of unconditional love, I have fallen well short of that elevated state any number of times. So, I ask, what do you do with a patient who is a royal pain-in-the-ass?

Paul was a functional sociopath. He had been a drug addict for fifteen years and had lived on the street. He trusted no one and viewed people only in terms of his ability to put one over on them. If he got what he wanted from you, you were a sucker, and if he didn't you were a useless S.O.B. He was a bigot, a bully and an ill-mannered boor, but he had AIDS and he needed help.

It was necessary for me to become very clear about what my responsibility was in this situation. I decided I was not there to teach manners, spirituality, or to punish or to judge. I was there to provide compassionate and comprehensive care to a critically ill human being. Each time I called or visited Paul, I had to remind myself of my responsibilities and tell myself not to personalize some of his more unpleasant remarks, such as, "Faggots make me puke," when my real inclination was to at least educate him, if not throttle him.

I did provide Paul with what he needed and never betrayed my negative feelings toward him, but I must say, with some guilt, that his death did not cause me the same distress I felt when other people I worked with died.

Physicians are often seen as objective and intellectually sophisticated enough to be above stigmatizing particular patients. Not only does personal experience show this to be often untrue, a study reported in the *American Journal of Public Health* cites significant physician prejudice towards AIDS patients:

Physicians reported much less willingness to interact with an AIDS patient even when none of the interactions described would carry any risk for human immunodeficiency virus (HIV) transmission.

Public attitudes toward AIDS represent primarily
a social issue. However, physician attitudes concern-
ing AIDS patients carry important health care ramifications. We found that the AIDS diagnosis carries emotional charge and elicits judgmental, negative evalu-
ations about the patient even by health care providers.
(Vol. 77, July, 1987, p. 789)

So here we are. Obviously our choice of caregiver as a
vocation or avocation implies we are concerned and gener-
ous. But we may have been socially imprinted with certain
prejudices that can subvert our aim of improving the health
and quality of life of people in need. How can we move
beyond prejudice?

The first step is to take a deeply searching but nonjudg-
mental personal inventory of the feelings we have toward
other groups of people. It is important to write this down
in order to see our feelings as they go from the general to the
particular. Just sit down and start writing whatever comes
to mind, for example:

I hate gay men. Gay men are effeminate. Gay men try
to have sex with all the men they meet. Gay men are
immoral. No, I have never had a bad experience with
a gay man but everyone knows...etc., etc.

Stay with the inventory until all of the connections
with the group have been exhausted.

Look for a trusted person such as a counselor with
whom to verbalize the feelings you have acknowledged.
The person you choose should be open-minded and non-
judgmental to create an atmosphere of trust in which
feelings can be shared openly. A professional might pro-

vide some constructive feedback, but any caring and trustworthy listener will provide the opportunity for self-examination and self-education about the stereotypes you have internalized.

Finding an environment in which you can interact, perhaps on social or community issues, with members of groups with which you have difficulties can be extremely helpful. A health care worker who connects to a largely gay-run AIDS support organization will soon recognize that gay people are non-threatening, and are as human and "mainstream" as anyone else. Visiting a drug-counseling center, or attending open Alcoholics Anonymous or Narcotics Anonymous meetings, will open your mind about substance abusers.

I have learned from my own experience that when we are consciously aware of feelings that were once hidden, the masks that keep us from genuinely relating to others disappear, and we find another human being not so unlike ourselves.

6

RESPONSE-ABILITY

By Rabbi Joseph Gelberman, Ph.D.

ABBI JOSEPH GELBERMAN has a congregation in New York City and New Jersey. Out of his belief in a need for dialogue between religions, he joined with a Catholic priest, a swami, and a Protestant minister to found The New Seminary where he trains Interfaith ministers. Rabbi Gelberman has a doctorate in psychology.

I've always thought that, in general, every person should be an actor and not a reactor. But when it comes to counseling a dying person, you have to react, not act. It doesn't matter what I think but rather, what this person needs. If I find this person is religiously oriented and happens to be Jewish, then I respond to that. I come in with prayers and words that I know are meaningful to that person. For example, if I leave a sick bed, instead of saying,

"I hope you feel better tomorrow," I say something in Hebrew. So when they hear this, they are connected with thousands of years of tradition. Just like when you travel somewhere and are in a strange place, and let's say you are Jewish, and all of a sudden somebody approaches you and says, "Shalom, my friend." Suddenly, there's a connection. In death, there's this same connection. When you really get sick, you go back to your children or relatives.

I use phrases or use prayer that is meaningful. Or, if I am with a person who is not religious, I do something else. For example, I was visiting a person who was dying of AIDS. He was not a religious person but his mother invited me over to say some prayers. I didn't say the prayers because I knew it would not help him. He was angry at God at that moment, he was angry at the synagogue, the Rabbis and everything in the world. So, I just tried to be a human being, a friend to touch. Sometimes I'd say something, or I'd say nothing and just look in his eyes. Once in awhile he'd open his eyes, and we'd make a connection. You have to be the reactor and respond. That's all you can do. You have to figure out what they need and sometimes they'll tell you. But it's important not to give them something they don't need. It's an art. The first thing I do when I come in is make eye contact. I try to convey through my eyes that I'm here as an ambassador of love and understanding and that I'm here for them. Then I wait for them to make the first move. I wait until the person wants to shake hands with me. If there is no move made, then I sit down and I try to get the family involved.

I ask, "Has so-and-so been here? Are you comfortable? Do you need something?" And little by little, you either make the connection or you don't. And if I don't make the connection, which is a great possibility, I just let it go. My first rule is: don't ever force anything on a sick person. You can only help them if they want to be helped. Especially when it comes to spritual matters.

If someone asks, "Why is God doing this to me?" I would say, "That's a good question. I don't know." Again, I would have to know the person to answer this question. My answer to myself is that God is not doing it, but if the sick person is not on that level and they feel God is doing everything, then this answer is not going to help. So the answer is, "You know, that's a really good question, let's talk about it. What makes you think God is doing this? And why do you think God would do this to you?" This often helps them open up. They may say, "Well, I have done this wrong," and maybe they need to confess. Then you have to respond without antagonizing them or denying their particular belief. It's important not to turn them off and risk severing the connection. You have to go along with what they're doing and create a dialogue and trust.

Another thing to remember as a general rule is that you're not going to settle the whole problem in one session. You don't need to be forceful or try to save the person. Just go there as a friend or as a healer.

I remember in the beginning when I started all this, there were many inappropriate things that I did. I would come in with this big title and say the prayers, and I would know how to argue with the person and it was so wrong! They're too weak to argue, and sometimes, they're too humble. You know, the Rabbi says something and they accept it. But just because they accept it doesn't mean it's right. Usually, they're frightened and angry. And why not? They're suffering.

One man I visited a few years ago was known all his life as a very calm, outgoing, beautiful and loving person. All of a sudden he gets sick, and he hates his wife and children and the whole world. So what's going on there? What happened all those years? He was faking it. He learned that it was good to be nice and it worked for him, but now when he was dying he started resenting all that. The real person came out at age seventy-one. He totally changed. Another personality altogether. So it must have been there all along. He was hiding it. Where was this personality all along? All of a sudden, he felt, "I'm sick and I'm angry!" I see that quite often. He was angry with me, too. You have to accept them however they are. I'm praying that when my time comes, I'll still love.

You have to be a healer for those few minutes, however long you're there. What's a healer? A healer is one who sees the suffering of the other, feels the suffering of the other, and tries to find in himself, either through words or through action, what might serve as a medication for the other. Again, connection. Because what is dying to begin with? We are cut off. But if we can feel, "I'm really not cut off, I'm still loved," then dying is just like going to sleep with total peace of mind and harmony. I've seen that, too.

You can prepare during your life in order to feel that peace and harmony at the end. I'm preparing myself that way. I'm preparing myself by eliminating anger, jealousy, hostility, all the deadly emotions, and fear is the deadliest of all. You can prepare yourself for death. That's where prayer comes in and that's where meditation comes in. Try to keep the mind in balance and accept both the good and the bad, the joys and the sorrow, the light and the darkness, the ugly and the beautiful, because you know it's all one, and therefore life and death are also one. They are different manifestations of the same thing.

What will happen when I die? I'd rather be concerned with what's happening while I'm still alive. That is my concern. What's happening today? To be alive is to be aware and to rejoice every moment.

I can look at the way you walk, the way you talk, your form. I also feel a part of your soul somehow, which is very different. I feel that, and I connect to that. I don't have to see you ever again, but I'll still know that you're a part of my life. With some people, you can make that connection.

The other thing is humor. We know that it has been medically established that humor is a tremendous help for healing, for getting well. I'm good at that. Almost anything can trigger a joke for me. Sometimes I'll make up a joke. There again, I would have to know the person and then I could make them laugh somehow.

If I meet the kind of person who expects me to do something, to make it all right, I try not to disappoint them. For example, there is a lady who is not too well, and she calls me almost every other day. She used to be a client of mine about five years ago. When she really needs help, she calls me. And I know her well enough to know that all she needs from me is some magic. If she's expecting a postal card from somebody, I tell her she'll get it. She may never get it, but as far as I'm concerned, my job is to keep her in that belief. "The Rabbi said I'll get it." That's what she needs to hear and I have to respond to that. That's what hope is.

A different kind of person would ask me, "What do you mean, how do you know?" That kind of person wouldn't believe me, so there would be no point in trying to build up hope in them. They would always be doubting, they would be angry if my promises didn't materialize.

There's another story about this old lady who was coming to me twice a year for years, and she was terribly attached to me and she really thought I was God. One day, I said, "You know Fanny dear, you know I'm really not God." She said, "But to me you are." There's no way I can change that and why should I? That's all she had. All she had was me. So, should I take that away from her? And the fact is that she was most interesting. The very day she died, she had used up all her money that day. Some people plan it; they do know when they're going to die. The point is, I have no right to destroy beliefs, especially in a dying person. You have to be a man of all seasons. On the other hand, if a young, healthy person had that kind of attachment to me, I would try to talk them out of it.

When a person is dying, something in me is dying too, because we are all one. Who is that person dying? Who is that person who is hungry? Who is that person who is joyous? Who is that person who is killing? Who is that person who is being killed? We are all one. It's the simplest concept and the most difficult one in the world. That's why in Judaism the most important part of any affirmation or any prayer is, GOD IS ONE. So are we all one. That would be my definition of human. A human being is one who understands the oneness of it all. That I, and that person in China, in Japan, in the Gulf, in Iran, the killers and the lovers, the young and the old, the men and the women, the rich and the poor, and the sick and the healthy—IT'S ALL ME!

When someone is dying, I am experiencing something that is going to happen to me later on, but it's also my experience in a way. If I can feel that way, and yet not feel it, that's the ideal—that connects us. Because if I feel it totally, then I'll go with them, but who's going to be helped by that? They have to go. I don't have to go yet. But what I'm saying is that a part of me is also leaving with them.

After a death, something is missing. That's why in every religion we have a memorial to remind us. The person is gone and you miss him. How much? Hopefully, not too much because it is going to interfere with your life. If I am mourning for the rest of my life, then I actually died with the person, but I wasn't buried. There is a man in my congregation whose wife died and he's been mourning for years now. He died with her. What can you say to a dead person? I'm there for him. I just listen, but there is nothing I can tell him. Maybe eventually he'll come out of it, but he's not here, he's there. At first I went down and spent a lot of time with him, but now I only go maybe once a month. I call him and I know the connection will still be there. I know at this point there is nothing I can do except to be there.

To be professional is to learn how to respond without losing yourself. A new caregiver can visit morning, noon and night, and burn themselves out. A story I tell in class is about two women who are having lunch, when one faints. They are the best of friends, so the other one faints to show sympathy. Sympathy is not helpful to you or your patient. Empathy, yes, but sympathy, no. You learn through experience to balance it, to put your ego aside.

When I come to a sick person, they are not interested in what I am. They are interested in that part of me that can be of help to them. Otherwise, why would they call me? So therefore, I have to find that part in me that will be helpful to them. I can do this by listening, examining, analyzing, meditating, and connecting.

You also have to know your limitations. Feeling like a martyr will build up a tremendous amount of resentment. Your patient will sense it too. You do whatever is necessary, and you do the best you can. You cannot make yourself sick emotionally, mentally, or physically. Who is helped by that? If it's an emergency, if the person is actually dying, all right, respond to the call. But otherwise, you make your calls, you do your job and you do whatever you have to do for yourself. What we call a "mensch," is the kind of person who knows himself, and by knowing yourself, you will know how to react to the other.

Caregivers need wisdom and knowledge—the two opposite sides of the tree of life. Knowledge is a certain amount of learning. Let's say I learned in school how to care for a person who is sick. That's knowledge. When it comes down to actually doing it, a certain amount of wisdom is required. When you have knowledge and wisdom, by definition, you are love. One without the other is not always loving. When you combine the two it equals love.

I'm not afraid of death, but I'm not waiting for it. I'm not excited about the concept. I would love to stay here as long as I can. I want to be healthy and well.

I talk about how I would feel if I became seriously ill, but it's something that I have no way of testing or proving until it happens. I only know me the way I know me now. If I got really sick, I would be frightened. I hope so. When I go to a wedding and the groom is nervous, I tell him it's a good sign. Because it's meaningful to you. If I don't care if I die, then life is not meaningful. I don't want to die, but when I do, I hope I go with a smile on my face and kiss the universe goodbye.

7
AN OPEN MIND

By Lesley Sanchez, L.P.N.

LESLEY SANCHEZ, who is studying for her R.N., had not yet entered nursing school when she began working with terminal patients and their families. Her account from the brand new caregiver's view illustrates that sometimes "not to know" can be a state of mind worth cultivating.

I think I went into this work because I was trying to find something meaningful for me. I volunteered at the center and took their nurse's training program on working with terminal patients. Although I wasn't a nurse yet, I knew I wanted to work with dying patients. It felt right. The center training helped a lot, but I was still scared when I went to meet my first patient. I hadn't seen anyone die before and I hoped my nervousness didn't show.

I'll never forget that first experience with Madeline. She was divorced with two teen-aged daughters and she wasn't comfortable having a stranger in the house. Still, she needed help with the girls and she wanted someone to do macrobiotic cooking, which was my specialty. So I moved in to stay for awhile. I sensed how wary Madeline was. I think I would probably have felt the same way, so I didn't act too forcefully. I didn't try to take over. I never changed anything in her house in any way.

I went in not knowing what to expect and let her tell me what she wanted. I didn't want to take away what little control she had left. When she realized I wasn't going to change her lifestyle, she began to feel comfortable enough to trust me. She just wanted peace around her, so I tried to fit into her environment. After she seemed to accept me, I began to do things for her that I felt would make her more comfortable or lighten her burden a little. I massaged her back and played some transcendental meditation tapes for her.

Even after I was with her for a few weeks, I never interfered with what was happening. I would allow her to go through whatever she needed to go through without trying to make it "better." I never said, "Oh, you'll feel better tomorrow." I just allowed her to have her pain and anger. I allowed her to be who she was without imposing my own feelings.

Madeline's sister was there a lot. We were the two people she seemed to accept. It was almost as if there was a gate around the house with a "Keep Out" sign on the front lawn. Occasionally, one or two people were allowed in for a few moments, but Madeline would get angry about visitors, so we respected her wishes by shuffling people out or asking them not to come. There was a real crisis going on in that house. The youngest child who was fifteen was very confused. Her mother had been sick for a long time so I don't think she had any idea that now her mother was dying. No one had talked to her about her mother's dying. She had not been included in it, so I tried to bring her into some of the other things that were going on in the house. Without saying too much, I wanted her to know that she was important and that her mother needed her.

The seventeen-year-old daughter was totally rebellious and angry at her mother for leaving her. She had to be responsible for her younger sister because they didn't have a father they could turn to for help. She seemed to be very bitter and didn't want to be a part of anything.

I talked to a center counselor and to one of their nurses who specialized in family communication because I felt I wanted to change the situation. But in the long run, their relationships stayed the same. That was frustrating at first, but I did accept the fact that you can't make people do anything they don't want to do.

There was so much going on in that house and I knew I had to be as calm as I could be. I wore many hats during that time, but I knew clearly that I was there for the patient above all.

I saw all the stages of dying that you learn about—the anger, the denial, the bargaining, the depression. In this particular case, the last stage, acceptance, was never reached. My initiation into the field, I think, brought me some intense learning lessons.

My next case taught me more. Fortunately, I was not the only person on that case. I worked with a team of nurse's aides. It was tough because the family seemed to be looking to me to be the daughter they never had. At times, it seemed as if they cared more about me than they did about the patient. There was a great deal of anger there as well. The wife was taking care of her mother-in-law, whom she had never liked. The mother-in-law was a frail, elderly and confused woman who was dying. On this second case, I made the mistake of becoming too involved with the family. It was a great lesson for me. I learned that it is not appropriate to divulge too much of your own personal life, that there has to be a certain amount of professional detachment.

People are very needy when someone is dying. I learned that you can't be there for everyone in the same amount. The patient has to be the main focus. It was tough for the family because they didn't want her to go on without any real quality in her life. They didn't want her life prolonged and they were not pushing food on her. It was a real dilemma for everyone on the case. She was a hospice patient, so I talked to the hospice about her nutritional needs. They certainly were not going to come in with tubes to give nourishment, but she did need to be fed when she was hungry. We had to go against what the family was saying. I didn't want to dehydrate the patient, so we would give small amounts of food and water. Sometimes you have to decide what is right and just do it.

Very rarely did I ever have problems with the patient. It seems to be the family dynamics that complicate the care. Most families are frightened and you have to step back and assess the situation. I tried to encourage the family members who really wanted to help, while not faulting those who didn't want to be included. You have to keep your eyes and ears open. You have to listen a lot to assess what's going on. In this second experience I learned more balance. "Grandma" as we called her, did die peacefully. That experience left me feeling a good deal older.

My experience with the following case, which I refer to as "the angry husband," matured me even more. Dave was angry from the minute I met him. His wife was dying, and he was feeling harassed by the responsibilities of the house. His daughter, a young woman in her twenties, was no help to him at all. The wife had always done everything in the house, taking care of his clothes, the shopping and the meals. Dave was a rather successful businessman, and now his entire schedule had been disrupted. He had to learn to wash his clothes, go food shopping, and do all the things his wife would normally do. His anger was compounded by all the strangers in his house and, unfortunately, I became the brunt of this anger. He was angry about everything I did. If I moved a tissue box out of place, he would burst into a fit of rage.

Finally, one day I had taken as much as I could tolerate from him. I said to him, "I'm here to take care of your wife and to make sure that she has as much quality of life as possible. I will help you in any way I can support you, but I am not here to take abuse from you." I tried to help him see what his anger was about. He sat down and had a long cry and we talked. He needed to talk about his wife's death and how difficult it was for him to begin to make funeral arrangements while she was still alive. We developed a bond of trust after I took the time to recognize his pain. I learned that you're not helping the person if you just take abuse, but attacking back is no solution either.

After Dave's wife died, he was very apologetic and grateful to me. In fact, he took the whole team of nurse's aides out to dinner and gave a long speech that he had written to express his gratitude.

What I've learned over the years is that there is not much you can say to someone when you're not in their position. You can be there to help them through it. You can try not to take away from what little they can do for themselves. You can't change things for them. You can't project your needs onto them. I just let people say and do what they need to do. I try to go there without any expectations about how it should be or how I want it to be. I try to remember that this is another person like me.

I read somewhere that people in the Mayan civilization had a way of addressing one another. When they met, the greeting was an hello to "another myself." So, I think about my patients as "another myself." I think about how I'd want to be treated. I remember that I'm in someone else's domain. They're letting me in.

I try not to make the patient feel that I'm talking behind his or her back. I think they deserve that courtesy. I prefer to wear my own clothes instead of going in a uniform. The medical approach doesn't seem to serve as well, unless there is pain medication involved. I think the key is that people are in their own homes and should be allowed to make their own choices. Of course, those choices should be educated ones. For instance, if their pain is acute and they are afraid of taking medicine for fear they'll be "out of it," you might call someone in to explain more about the medicine and the control they can exercise in terms of dosage.

The gifts I have received from working with dying people are many, but most of all I've learned more about myself. I can't say I won't be frightened when it's my turn to die, but I think I understand it a little better. I think I would not try to fight it. I have seen the experience of death as being like birth. You go out and you come in.

I feel the hardest task for me as a caregiver is to find the balance between being personally involved and being professional. My aim is to be able to be with people, recognizing what's happening, what they want. I want to feel for them, but not take it on myself; to be empathic but not overly sympathetic. I want to go to people with an open heart and an open mind.

8

JOURNEYING SIDE BY SIDE

By Charles Lochner, M.A., M.S.

C HARLES LOCHNER *has recently accepted the position of executive director of The Center for Help in Time of Loss. This chapter is taken from a talk given for the 1989 convention of The New Jersey Association of Professional Counselors.*

I am a therapist who works primarily with people who are attempting to negotiate that often lonely passage through death and loss. I like to refer to it as the journey through grief. My role is to accompany people on this journey. What I am is a companion, a fellow wayfarer. As I often tell my clients in my introductory session, I am simply going to walk with them for a little while. Along the way we will talk and break the bread of our lives. We will visit the valley of darkness where nothing will be clear and all will seem as if it is for naught. We will share the story of our pain and ultimately make friends with it. This pain that makes us die inside, if befriended, will also bring us new life.

Much of what I share with you will be an invitation to take that journey within to befriend and honor every part of you, especially the lonely place of pain within your own life. It is crucial that we find a way to do this: our very capacity to heal depends on it. It is only when we have embraced our own lives that we can genuinely accompany others into their lives. In his book *Easter & Eden*, Dr. Anthony Padovano states that only those who go through the "right" experiences know what to be and say to others in their hour of need. I believe that every adult has been through the "right experiences" — the problem is that we often don't tend to them. We pay no attention and thus, it is as if we have not had them.

Three months after her twenty-year-old daughter's suicide, a client of mine was brought to a hospital for psychiatric evaluation. She was experiencing panic brought on by a "nightmare" that wouldn't end. When she was finally seen by a psychiatrist she told him of her agony. His response to her was that she had better stop acting like an idiot or else she would have to be hospitalized.

I do not know this doctor, but I am sure he has had years of training at fine academic institutions. Somewhere on some wall, undoubtedly, are his diplomas and certificates testifying to years of hard work. But in this case, none of that helped him. He said the wrong thing. He was not there for her.

I am sure that this physician had some losses in his life simply because we all do. You don't have to experience the death of a loved one to know the land of loss. In all of our lives there are many little losses. Dying, on some level, is a daily act. All along the way, in countless little and big ways, we are asked to let go. Perhaps in his life there had even been a major loss. I don't know. But this much I do know: whatever loss was in this doctor's life, he did not pay attention to it. He had missed the point. No one had ever helped him to see that his power to heal was hidden within his own pain. He never learned how to befriend and honor the very experience of his own life.

To be present for others demands that I be present for myself. To help someone else embrace their own pain requires that I honor my own. I can guide and accompany you on this journey through grief because, on some level, this journey has been my own.

Counseling is about companionship. We are companions for a journey. Counselor and client, doctor and patient, teacher and student are simply words we use—just labels. But the truth is that we're in this together. I use the word "journey" to describe counseling because the experience of counseling is often diverse and unpredictable. We professionals have developed ways to control this experience. We have a prolific vocabulary of terms to describe and diagnose what goes on inside and between the counselor and client. The information and technology of counseling is expanding every day. The load of junk mail that I receive each week attests to this fact. But all of the jargon and techniques do not describe the actual experience.

I write about my daily encounters with clients in my journal, trying to capture that experience:

> You have invited me to share the painful loneliness of your grief. You come into my office half-dazed, barely able to speak. You sit there broken apart by the death of the one you love. I look into your eyes and catch your anger and fright. We begin our conversa-

tion—I have my questions, my professional protocol to follow—but it all means nothing. My walls are covered with diplomas and certificates creating the illusion that I might know something that you don't. But I don't know that magic something. Every part of me wants to rescue you from the darkness of death, but I cannot. And so, I try to neutralize the trauma. I tell you that what you are feeling is very "normal." I tell you that others have experienced similar tragedies and have survived. I point out the "landmarks" on the path of grief. I speak about sleeping problems—too much or too little; the depression, the shock and anger.

I have done my homework. The darkness is not really dark. And, although a part of you needs to know this information, another part couldn't care less. You challenge me and my smug learning. On your angry days you dare me to enter the darkness with you. And on those other days, overwhelmed by sadness, you wordlessly ask me to be with you. Feeling my own powerlessness, my own loneliness, my own fears—I take my stand with you. On some days I do it well. On other days my own brokenness is too deep. Those are the days in which you sense my distance.

Working with you forces me to think about the darkness surrounding death. The despair that destroys all joy; the death that makes us die inside; the loneliness of having no one there; the angry resignation felt when no one cares. This is what you invite me to share. You ask me to leave my learning at the door of your soul and bid me enter the darkness with you. My first reaction is to run, for the darkness I fear in you is really part of me. Your loneliness and angry agony, your desolation and despair, belong to me too. So what are we to do?

How does one walk in darkness? It seems to me that the "answer" lies in the darkness, not away from it.

This is a difficult truth to embrace. Part of our despair comes from realizing that there is no exit from the darkness. We get that feeling whenever we acknowledge that the hurt is so deep it cannot be undone. The one we counted on is lost forever. It is precisely this darkness that we must enter. We want a way out—a way of loving without losing.

So, we are invited to go on a journey. Along the way we will talk and get to know each other. Although I go with you as a guide, there is a sense that this particular journey is new for me because it is framed by the context of your life. You will not simply reveal yourself to me—you will reveal who I am to myself. If I am really with you, this revelation will be inescapable. Some of it will be painful. But if I have paid attention to the pain in my own life, I will not be frightened by it. I will not all of a sudden tell you that there is something wrong with you, that what you are feeling you should not be feeling. I will not attempt to deflect your feelings so that I do not have to embrace my own.

I have a client who visits me weekly. She is a young woman who originally sought my help because a very close friend had died. She actually came to see me because her parents were worried about her. During the course of therapy her mother died. Sometimes, when this young woman visits my office we simply sit in silence. Every now and then she will look up and our eyes will lock. Nothing will be said verbally, but if one can be quiet enough inside, one can hear the word of pain that is being shared. Like companions on a journey, we sometimes travel in silence lost in our thoughts yet knowing that we are not alone. She said to me one day at the end of a session, "You know, it helps me that you sit with me and allow me to be quiet. I come here and try to face my pain. Knowing you're there helps me to do that."

Being there is our task. Whether it be a person in grief or a student trying to decide on a college, a man in mid-life trying to define himself or an unmarried woman attempting to bridge the loneliness of her life, our first task is to be there. We are not there when we try to talk them out of their feelings, telling them to grow up and face life and stop acting like idiots. We're also not there when we are too tired, burnt out or have not tended to our own lives.

Being there requires a passion for living. A passion that allows us to love and embrace life on its own terms complete with its death and dying, its laughter and pain, its love and loneliness. Being there demands that we love the fool within us—the one who goofs off and makes silly mistakes, the one who sins and the one who destroys our neatly ordered life.

Being a counselor can at times be a "heady job." People come to us to seek our wisdom and we are placed in the role of the shaman. The problem is that we might begin to believe what they say about us. Forgetting what the Oracle at Delphi said of Socrates—that he was the wisest man in Athens because he knew he did not know— we think we know.

A number of years ago, I was teaching a seminar on death and dying at a local college. During one of our many discussions, a student asked me why I do the work I do. I could see that behind the question was her suspicion that I must be completely crazy to be working around death. Looking her right in the eye, I said in jest that if I walked with death enough—if I studied it, touched it, spoke about it and so forth—then maybe I would not have to do it myself. I would thereby escape my own dying. Well, you and I know what is said about things told in jest: they often contain much truth. The temptation to substitute our learning for living is always present and when given in to, that temptation will take the healing out of helping.

When people invite you to journey with them through the valley of darkness, they are not asking for another technician to join them. They are not asking your Ph.D., your M.S. or M.D. to join them, but the one who has lived and died a thousand deaths. They want you because what they are asking for is company for the journey.

Working around death has helped me to focus on living in a more direct way. It has sharpened my sensitivity toward life. It has helped me to live *now* and has taught me not to waste precious time. The dying have taught me that death is not frightening in itself, but rather the thought of dying without ever having lived is frightening.

I feel that in some ways counseling is an invitation to my clients to be fully alive. For this reason, counseling requires a passion for living. By passion I mean the capacity to feel deeply and throw yourself into living. A passion that enables us to honor every part of our lives, even the broken parts.

So much of a counselor's training is aimed at bringing order out of chaos. That is why we have tests and measurements, diagnostic categories and theories of development. No one will dispute the goal of order. We have to know what we are talking about in order to communicate. However, we need to be aware that none of that can take our place. The invitation to be alive, the invitation to our clients to accept and love themselves, must be embedded in our spirit. Therapists, counselors, and caregivers need to ask themselves: What do my clients sense from me? What do they learn? Do my students and clients go away with an awareness that life, despite its broken places, is ultimately worth living? Do they go away with a sense that nothing within them is unacceptable? That they can love the whole thing, even the mess they're in?

Several years ago I wrote this poem about the need to love ourselves:

I may be able to speak
with great wisdom and understanding
but if I do not love myself,
I understand nothing.

I may talk a good game
I might know a lot about life
but if I do not know that I am loved—
then, I know nothing.

I may be a person of strong faith
be able to believe with certainty
but if I do not believe in myself—
then I believe in nothing.

I may be a person who is always giving,
always caring about others' needs—
but if I do this, because I can't
allow myself to need—
then, my caring is crippled—
it does me no good.

I love myself when I am patient
when I can be quiet with waiting—
not rushing my joy
nor denying my pain.

I am my own friend—
with kindness for free—
I own what I am
  my anger and hurt
  my laughter and love
they never own me.

Although my life may be fragile
  with failure—
I am not afraid
I do not hold on to what has gone wrong—
for me living is now and
love is today.

Over and over again, the task is to make friends with all that is within us. So much energy is spent in excluding from our awareness the difficult feelings associated with our brokenness. We tell ourselves that we are okay but never really feel it. To keep our fragile balance we also try to stay away from people who remind us of ourselves. The problem facing me as a counselor is that I often do not have control over who I see and even if I do, it is not until I get into the counseling that I discover that this client carries the same burden I have struggled with for years. Somehow they find us! They sit with us and in their life's agony I see my own.

I will do everything by the book. My diagnosis and treatment plan will be right on target. Everything will be in place but me. And then, after all of this does not work, I will call them resistant and suggest that they see another therapist. For part of our task is to recognize when we cannot help another because our own resistance is too great.

Counseling is not a profession for the innocent. It is, rather, for those who are guilty. Guilty of having lived and loved. Guilty of living with the contradictions of failure and faith, love and loss. It is for those who can laugh at themselves and who can understand that we are all way-farers. It is for those whose passion for living leads them to a profound acceptance of life in its totality.

It is not that we have the answers that make us healers, but that we share the questions. What makes us able to help is that we have also learned to love the questions. How does one walk in darkness? By making friends with it.

A young father came to see me one day. His wife had recently died leaving him to care for two young boys ages five and seven. He was broken apart by the death of the one he loved. He wept as he told me of the journey he had been on—the days and nights spent in a hospital, the unanswerable questions of his two young boys, his disbelief that this could be happening at all. One of his concerns was that he felt he was going crazy because of the overwhelming strength of his feelings. He found it hard to control himself, especially in front of his children. He was concerned that by not being strong, by not keeping his feelings inside, he was somehow making it worse for his children.

The task was to walk with him far enough so that he could see that his suffering bore witness to his great love, a love that was essentially a gift. Seeing it from this vantage point transformed the meaning of his tears. They did not mean that he was crazy, they meant that he had loved. As he became more comfortable with his pain, his children became more comfortable with theirs. Children and adolescents do not need answers as much as they need adults who are clearly in love with life—a love that is broad enough to hold within its embrace all the contradictions of living. In my view, a counselor is one who in spirit exemplifies the risk of loving life in this way. Such a love demands a certain passion.

But it is just this passion that spawns the gift of compassion. Only those who go through the right experiences know what to be and what to say to others in their time of need. It is because I have faced this within myself that I can wait with you when you cannot find the words.

Part 2

Caring for the Caregiver

9
TAKE GOOD CARE OF YOURSELF

By Lois Lorenz, M.S.W., C.S.W., ED.S.

L OIS LORENZ *is director of training and education for The Center for Help in Time of Loss. She is a social worker with a varied background in counseling and education, and has led training programs for dozens of hospitals and hospices.*

When asked to write a chapter on preventing burnout, I found myself simply restating all the articles I have read on stress reduction or rehashing material covered in workshops I have attended. After giving the subject more thought, I decided to make the assumption that most experienced health care workers have the knowledge of what they "should" do for themselves to reduce stress and improve job satisfaction. For the newer worker, this information is readily available [see bibliography -Ed.]. Instead, I would rather look at some of the influences, internal and external, that we allow to serve as obstacles to using stress-reduction and self-nourishing techniques. In place of suggesting "how to," I will offer some thoughts for understanding "why we don't." Identifying some of these influences may provide a first step toward doing unto ourselves as we try to do unto others: to nourish, to respect, to care.

In high school I was very much a fan of the writer and popular philosopher Ayn Rand. I devoured her books, *The Virtue of Selfishness* and *Atlas Shrugged*. Now, thirty years later, I remember few details from these books. Their theme, however, was a strong and proud statement advocating the right of individuals to place themselves at the very top of their own priority list, an affirmative statement that "I matter!" and that I should be willing to take action to defend this position. As I recall, this stance was defended by the author as both forming the basis of a system of ethical morality which would benefit mankind, and as a sound principle of personal mental health.

I read Ayn Rand in the 1950's. Today I read articles on burnout and stress reduction which suggest that I should matter to myself, but the message is generally presented in a gentle, inoffensive, almost apologetic tone. Rand's novels were, for a good part of my adolescent years, the basis of my philosophy of life. Today, having worked for over twenty years in health care, I often experience taking care of myself as an ongoing process of self-assessment, vigilantly looking for signs of overwork, stress, or (oh, that dreaded term) burnout. How did something that at fifteen seemed an inalienable right become a hard-won and often elusive necessity? In reviewing this process, I speak for myself but offer what I hope may be a useful framework from which others can evaluate their own experience.

In the 1960's times changed. Society developed, at least for a decade, a new definition of what constituted an ethical position of life. I attended a college during that time at which it was fashionable, if not socially mandatory, to profess socially-conscious views, putting the needs of the masses before those of the individual. Our intense conversations in Greenwich Village coffee houses no longer focused on the virtues of selfishness, but instead extolled joining workers chopping sugar cane in the Cuban fields, risking arrest at a peace march or civil rights demonstration, or helping the poor right here at home, in New York City. Upon graduation I did my part, signing on as a social caseworker for the New York City Department of Social Services. Assigned to a territory rife with poverty and rioting, I saw the needs of the poor firsthand and wondered about the ethics of buying a new dress for myself when another woman could barely afford food for her family. (I solved my dilemma and soothed my conscience by sneaking back into "my territory" at night, to give my used clothes to some of my selected welfare clients—those that wore my size and wouldn't tell.)

At the welfare office in the mid-60's, burnout was experienced in terms of witnessing and experiencing (even vicariously) the unfairness or inequality in the societal system. Inequality was defined in terms of money, opportunity, and material possessions. Solutions were primarily seen as political—organizing the poor or changing the political system.

The lives of the poor didn't stop at five o'clock but my contact with them did. My world after work was middle-class and different from theirs. I picked causes with an environmental focus in which to invest my volunteer hours and felt, in some small measure, that I was making a positive contribution to humanity. I felt concern for individual clients but did not identify with them. I also had the ability to separate myself physically from them each night. In that decade the plight of the world seemed an overriding ethical concern, but as an individual I could still feel a sense of personal morality, picking my own cause and still having a personal life separate from my work.

Setting the client's needs as the highest priority was a clear norm in social-work education in the climate of the late 1960's. Entering graduate school, you quickly learned that the ability and willingness to do this was a significant mark of the true professional. Yes, skill development mattered too, but it was rarely seen as a substitute for a high level of personal caring (termed "professional commitment"), which included the willingness to give of yourself and help others. In a profession in which salaries have traditionally been low, rewards must come from the gratification of altruism, of helping another in need, and from recognizing that through your efforts growth and change in another have occurred. "When have I given enough?" was a question I never heard asked. Was it when the work day ended? When the client "got better," a concept for which there was rarely objective criteria? Or, when the worker could give no more? Confronted with the often overwhelming problems that clients faced, I wondered if I could ever give enough. Yet, my graduate school courses not only seemed to encourage workers to extend themselves, but rarely, if ever, gave concrete guidelines for when or how to set limits on giving. For myself, and probably for others, this was the beginning of a process of sacrifice-conditioning under the guise of professionalism and commitment.

I recently took a course in cardio-pulmonary resuscitation. When asked by the students how long to continue CPR on an unconscious victim, the professor replied, "Until you can no longer continue from your own complete exhaustion." Do we sometimes have this CPR mentality about our clients' emotional needs as well?

About ten years ago, my career direction shifted to oncology and the concept of caring and giving took on new dimensions in a health care setting. I worked first in one of the early hospice programs in which the norms of caring, loving, and giving were deemed hallmarks to the program's success. Palliative care was in its early stages of development and pain relief was seen as being more effective when the patient received a high level of personal care and caring from family, volunteers and staff alike. And the concept worked. As caregivers learned to refine and employ these techniques, the quality of patients' lives did appear to improve. We learned to care and give care in these new ways and we received our reward. Our personal tendencies to care and be caring grew stronger with this reinforcement.

Hospice philosophy is sometimes criticized for the emphasis it places on relaxing barriers and role definitions between patients and staff. In my experience, personal caring has the potential to enrich the worker's job. Unending giving, however, can strip the life force slowly away. As the emotional component of palliative care becomes more sophisticated, we may be learning to set appropriate limits on caring without sacrificing the quality of patient care.

Working in health care can be a tricky business. Unlike welfare clients, cancer patients can be more like you and me. Not only could anyone get cancer, but these patients can live in your own community — you do not necessarily have to transport yourself to theirs. So, if they got it, you could get it too. And you run the risk of bumping into your patients after work at the supermarket or the post office. It is much harder to separate yourself here.

Patients who have cancer, generally, have needs around the clock. This is especially apparent when working in terminal care where the timing of a patient's death is unpredictable. Before the hospice movement, the saying, "Not on my shift" characterized the staff's fear and discomfort in dealing with a patient's death. The hospice movement flipped the coin to, "Please, on my shift." Caregivers who have grown fond of a particular patient or family may very much want and need to be present during the dying process, but this requires being on-call in their free time— being prepared to rush to the patient's side day or night much as family members do. The alternative is to miss some, or all, of these important moments in order to protect what is often preciously limited personal or family time. This scenario can be a classic lose/lose situation. You have to either be on-call at the expense of private time, or risk having no sense of closure. You really can't have it both ways. But what you *can* do, is make a conscious choice as to how much you are able to give on each case.

I still remember when I worked in a hospital setting, and came to visit a patient whom I had seen almost daily for six weeks and had known well for over a year before that. That morning a new patient was in "her" bed. In retrospect, I doubt that, even if called, I would have travelled the twenty miles back to the hospital in the very early morning hours when the patient died, but I never quite got to say my goodbyes. By the next morning the staff had changed and there was no one to talk to about when or how she had died. Completing the dying process with at least selected patients can help caregivers deal with the multitude of losses they experience. What happens to the worker when too many of these processes are aborted?

Working in oncology and terminal illness can subject caregivers to a subtle form of guilt for successfully taking care of themsleves and being healthy. Similar to the "survivor guilt" family members experience after a death, healthy workers can sometimes feel guilty, vulnerable, or uneasy being in a setting in which so many others have, or have had, cancer. The caregiver may tend to over-give as a kind of irrational penance for being well, or as a magical ritual to remain that way: If I give enough, this surely cannot happen to me.

Caregivers witness the emotional and sometimes physical pain experienced by patients and family members which is frequently not alleviated at the end of their shift or working day. Consistently facing others' seemingly unrelieved pain can have a cumulative effect on the caregiver. It is often difficult to maintain the perspective that the family, whose pain we see and participate in, will one day be relieved, particularly when we will not be part of this extended healing process. Caregivers who are able to provide long-term bereavement follow-up have more opportunity to see the results of this natural process. Too often, we witness the mental pain a family experiences without seeing the recovery and full, rich lives which are possible as healing occurs. Without this firsthand, longer-term perspective, it is easy to begin to view life as a succession of endless sufferings.

I find it helpful to be around staff and volunteers who have suffered loss and recovered. They are living testimonials that recovery is possible. Remembering times when I have experienced loss and come through also brings me perspective when I am sitting with someone who believes there will never be reason to live again. There are also times when volunteering to help an individual move ahead in bereavement, or to lead a bereavement support group, may provide a healthy perspective that keeps me fresh and hopeful in my everyday work.

Another potential double-bind for the worker in oncology care is the frequent need to offer support groups or educational programs for patients and families during evening hours. Evening groups which cater to family members' working schedules often are better attended than daytime programs. Similarly, hospice and other volunteer training programs are often held after working hours. Workers may feel conflicting pulls between wanting to offer programs that provide them with challenge, diversity, and both personal and professional reward, and wanting to preserve personal and family time. These programs are often given on the staff's volunteer time, thus increasing the conflict between wanting to help, and wanting to limit how much of yourself and your time you are willing to give.

Hospice and some other terminal-care settings rely heavily on volunteer involvement for service delivery. Volunteers can be the shining stars of a program. They provide free service which might not otherwise be offered, plus those who volunteer are usually committed and delightful individuals, truly a pleasure to work with. However, working with volunteers often requires extra time for training, supervision, and support. For the worker this can be viewed as volunteer time from one's own commitment or as unpaid overtime. If it starts to feel like the latter, resentment is bound to build up. Yet, if a volunteer is giving their time willingly to your program, you may feel selfish by not wanting to give your extra time as graciously.

Another factor which may inhibit putting forth the effort to care for ourselves lies in the influence of our peers and the role models they provide. We frequently work with other professionals who take far worse care of themselves than we do—working long hours, taking on two jobs, eating poorly, smoking, and reserving little, if any, time for recreation, exercise, or refreshment. Despite the "fitness craze" of the past few years, most people feel a degree of pressure to conform to their peer group, feeling discomfort when seeming different than those around them. And there can be realistic negative social consequences. The non-smoker misses the comradeship of the lounge where staff gather for a smoke. Continuously refusing to share the pizza or sugar-coated donut holes can be attributed only so long to being on a diet. Social norms are changing but destructive habits in health care workers remain. The price of personal caretaking can be varying degrees of social isolation.

The United States champions the rugged individual, the man or woman who stoically faces adversity with neither a tear nor a whimper. Strength against all odds is seen as an ideal, while acknowledging even legitimate limitations may be defined as a weakness, "complaining," or simply undesirable behavior. Thus, caring for yourself is frequently interpreted not as a responsible act, but instead, as responding to a deficit in your personal makeup. The pressure can be fourfold: it may come from your own personal values or conditioning; from the supervisor who reviews your performance using these values; from peers who are threatened by, or oblivious to, caring for themselves; or from organizational norms that stress productivity regardless of workers' needs.

Just as society in the 1960's placed value on being a caregiver to the world without a thought for yourself, the 1980's may be seen as the decade of the super-achiever. No personal price is too great to pay to achieve the material goals which are flaunted in the media daily. For those who aspire to reach living standards espoused by the media, overtime or second jobs may be the norm. In a decade that values status and possessions above the individual, caring for oneself may seem to be an unaffordable luxury and rarely a top priority.

The amount and quality of research that has been done on both the need for stress management and techniques for implementing these principles is impressive. A source of true amazement, however, is the fact that this rapidly expanding body of knowledge, while reaching some sections of the corporate community, appears almost totally absent in the consciousness of health care administration, as reflected in their employee policies.

Relaxation training, exercise and healthy diet are principles taught to corporate executives and often made available to employees through lunch-hour or after-work programs. Despite the fact that the research on stress management generates from the health care and mental health systems, wellness for health care workers is rarely recognized by administration or even by workers themselves. The sad irony is that the mechanic will value and care for his tools far more effectively than most health care workers value their own most essential tool: their physical, emotional, and spiritual selves.

Perhaps the concrete—the plumber's wrench, the surgeon's hands—are understood and related to more easily than the abstract; the quality of concern and warmth that transforms health workers from technicians into artists or masters in their field. Without regular attention given to valuing and maintaining human qualities, we risk becoming assembly-line practitioners, or we end up by deciding to leave the field.

In my experience, the following norms exist in varying degrees within the traditional health care system:

- If it's scientific, it has value; if it's not scientific, it's worthless.

- "Cure" is our goal; "palliative care" is slowly gaining acceptance; "prevention" — could you define that one, please?!

- Doctors matter; ancillary staff should follow doctors' orders, be seen and not heard, and work hard at it.

Does working within these norms influence our attitudes about caring for ourselves? I think so. The value of the scientific approach is a strong norm in most health care settings, particularly in teaching hospitals and research centers. An important corollary is that conditions and results be measurable and validated. The more trials a drug has experienced or the longer it has been around within a scientifically-approved framework, the more acceptance it generally receives. Because of the time period involved in the scientific approach, change and its acceptance come slowly and cautiously.

Despite the scientific research being done to validate the techniques of stress reduction, the field remains relatively new in a system which values tradition and the status quo. To complicate the situation further, researchers feel that, although symptoms of stress can be measured, overall stress is often a very subjective experience and is therefore difficult to measure scientifically. Much of the research on stress reduction is done by non-physicians (psychologists, nurses, and social workers), again detracting from the health care system's willingness to accept the findings or recommendations. As caregivers working within the health care system, we are deeply influenced by this rigid point of view.

The second norm, stressing the importance of cure, overlooks the progressive stages of a pathological condition. It also suggests a quick answer or solution—take a pill, or at most a series of pills, and the condition will go away. To be most effective, self-care should fall within the preventive end of the spectrum, one seldom addressed by conventional medicine. When the condition becomes acute, its symptoms can be treated but the root of the problem, or the life changes needed for its alleviation, are rarely addressed beyond the physician giving, at best, lip-service advice. The remedy is devalued further by the fact that relatively few health care providers "practice what they preach," giving less credence to their recommendations.

Finally, the hierarchy which exists within the medical system can influence the health care provider's feelings of self-worth and worthiness to receive self-care. Physicians, while generally at the top of the hierarchy, may live by the beeper or patient's demands, neither of which take into consideration individual needs for refreshment, periodic separation from work, or self-nourishment. While this can be compensated to some extent by income, prestige, and time away, other members of the health care team may experience similar pressures with fewer rewards. Perhaps more importantly, working in a system in which your role may be undervalued can, over time, erode your feeling of self-worth. This can lead to chronic dissatisfaction with your profession, or cause you to work beyond realistic expectations in order to validate your role within the system.

I exercise regularly using tapes I've made of a popular aerobic class on television. One day the instructor gave a pep talk about the importance of continuing some form of exercise when away on even a two-week vacation, or risk suffering the consequences of lost fitness when you return. What a thought! A whole year's effort diminished in two short weeks of sloth! Can't we have any fun? Get away from the old, daily routine even for a short while? Well, we can, but there are consequences.

Nourishing the self is like maintaining physical fitness—it takes regular attention and effort, and in whatever form, it is lifelong. Overwhelming? Not necessarily so, although the likelihood is good that it will require some conscious changes in values and priorities. How severe these changes need to be depend on personal goals. While I may exercise thirty minutes a day, I have no aspirations to be a body-builder or marathon runner. Similarly, my self-care goals aim at being effectual yet still allowing me to live comfortably in everyday life.

Still, I have found that I need to set "Nourishing Myself" as a priority in my life and take active responsibility for following through with what needs to be done for me. It means challenging some traditional habits. I was brought up to eat meat, potatoes and vegetables; now I seldom eat meat and have learned gradually over fifteen years to plan diets and prepare food differently. It has meant some change in routine. I get up an hour earlier for meditation and exercise, which often means cutting time off of evening activities. However, the increased energy I get from this practice makes it worth it. And I have shifted priorities in socializing. Going out for a drink in a smoky bar with co-workers holds no attraction. This has sometimes meant making the effort to find alternative ways to maintain needed work relationships.

Changes need not be abrupt or dramatic, but can be integrated gradually into your life style by experimenting with what will work for you personally. But some changes will need to be made, and that requires a degree of commitment and willingness to make an extended effort over time to maintain new habits.

Does it sound like too much work? Is it really necessary? To me, the answer can be seen in terms of both valuing yourself for yourself and being willing to take responsibility to fine-tune yourself as a tool to help others. A dull tool may cut, but it will take progressively longer and, as it dulls more and more, the job will eventually become hacked and torn. A well-sharpened tool may require effort to maintain but it is a joy to use. Each person needs to decide the degree of compromise they're willing to tolerate for themselves. Seen in this context, caring for yourself need no longer be defined in terms of weakness, luxury, or selfishness, but rather as an essential part of the caring we wish to extend.

10

A WAY TO SAY GOODBYE

By Bonnie Teich, R.N.

BONNIE TEICH *has been in nursing for three years. She is with the Visiting Nurse Service in New York City.*

In nursing school there was hardly any preparation for working with terminal patients—maybe two classes and that was in my last year. It was really a lot of background and theory. So, it was devastating when I had my first terminal patient. He was an AIDS patient and I saw him deteriorate really quickly. I had been in nursing about a month. I had just graduated and joined the Visiting Nurses. I didn't know what to do. He really prepared me because he was prepared to die. He had accepted the fact that he was going to die, so he went very peacefully, at home with his friends and loved ones around him. I was running around frantic. It was really hard for me because I hadn't accepted it at all.

Now, I just let people decide how they want to deal with it and I support whatever they do. I just listen, and let them vent. I try to get them to talk about what they're feeling so that it's not all locked inside. That's really what I do, that's all I do. You have to develop a relationship with the patient, or it doesn't work. They won't talk to you, if you don't. It takes a long time. You have to develop trust, and it's hard.

I have found that it's hard for me to deal with people who are dying. Don't expect it to be easy, it's very difficult. I'm going through an experience now with a daughter and a mother. I've known this family for about five months. The patient had a stroke and was bedbound when she was admitted to me. She was somewhat paralyzed on one side. She had been a very active woman, and had done a lot of volunteer work. It took about four months to get her up and out of the house, and it was wonderful when we did.

She did very well until one day when I received a phone call from her daughter who lives with her and is very supportive. She told me her mother had been admitted to the hospital and was dying. She told me about her plans to sign the DNR (do not resuscitate) paper so the hospital wouldn't be liable. I sat and listened to her for an hour telling me how she came to this decision. She cried and I cried with her. She was just so strong about the whole thing. I wasn't strong about it myself. I was quite emotional, because I thought about my own mother. I don't think I could have taken care of my mother like this daughter did.

Her mother is still in the hospital. She is very uncomfortable and in a lot of pain, and I care about the quality of her life. It's very sad to go through all these things with the family. I just listen to the daughter and help her plan, because she's under a lot of pressure from the hospital to take her mother home. If her mother survives she'll have to go to a nursing home, which is another thing that I had to help her face.

Every single experience is so different, and my relationship is different with everybody each time. If I knew somebody for only a month and they died, I probably wouldn't be so affected, but the more I know people, the more I'm involved and the more it affects me. There is no planned way of how I handle it.

I would say to a new caregiver: Just be yourself. Don't worry about saying the wrong thing. Just be yourself, be there and be supportive. That's all you can do. It's not something you can prepare for. There is no way I can plan what I'm going to say or do. In my job as a visiting nurse, I'm going into a situation where there's an existing problem or crisis going on and I'm there to help. Ninety-five percent of the time they're responsive to your visit, so it's very easy because they're thankful for whatever you can offer them. You are somebody objective who can provide services and be supportive.

Most of all, I think you have to be real. If you say you're going to do something, do it! It's not unlike all relationships. You can't just walk in and say, "Hello, my name is Mrs. so-and-so, I'm here to take your blood pressure, goodbye, see you." You walk into people's houses. It's their domain.

When I saw my first AIDS patient (I'll call him Gary), I was very scared because I didn't know much about AIDS. I hadn't had any close relationships with gay men. I don't know what I expected, but he was a very normal guy who had normal feelings, a normal life and a normal job.

He was alert and oriented at that point. However, he had become so depressed he talked about ending his life. I thought in my head, "You have to be cool here, you can't flip." I was really panicking inside though. I didn't really know what to do. My mind was racing back to my psychiatric nursing text, suicide, page 365, what do I do? What I did do was just listen to him. Then I tried to find out if he had a plan or not, but he didn't. Then I sat and listened to him for an hour. He cried, he got angry, and then he seemed okay. I ran outside, got some fresh air and called the doctor. I told him what had happened and the doctor called him. After that, Gary seemed better and he never spoke about it again.

I saw Gary a lot but he was very hard to get to know. I knew him for six months before he started to open up. I would go in two or three times a week and just listen to him. It helped me to learn more about him. He talked about his life, his family and his lover. He talked about his inability to have sex at that point, which was very frustrating for him. He was so open and he taught me a lot. In the midst of all this, his lover began rejecting him. He didn't treat Gary well at all. Gary had three really close friends who supported him. He also had a nun, a buddy from the Gay Men's Health Crisis, who was very supportive. She did a lot of concrete things like laundry and cleaning the house.

He never lost his mind. He had multiple brain tumors, but he was alert until he died. I watched him become paralyzed. He couldn't eat. But I heard he died with incredible dignity. It was very sad the way I found out about his death. I went to his house and he was gone. I felt very sad because I was just all of a sudden cut off. None of his friends called me, and we were so close. It was just awful and I was really angry. I called the doctor, and then I met one of Gary's friends on the street. He apologized that no one had gotten in touch with me. It made me feel terrible because I thought I was so involved, and I was involved, but all of a sudden I was not part of it. A lot of times it's like that, though. No matter how much you care, or how much you think you're involved, you still represent the other side. You are considered a professional, not a friend. I think it's very hard for the caregiver.

A similar thing happened with another patient of mine. I adored this woman. She was so close to me and gave so much back. I just enjoyed her company very much. She called me up one morning and said she couldn't breathe. I called 911 emergency, and she went to the hospital. I went to visit her, and found out she had died. I couldn't get in touch with her daughter and nobody ever got in touch with me. I wanted to send a card and go to the funeral, but nobody ever said anything to me. I left messages on her family's answering machine to no avail. I didn't have a chance to say goodbye to her. I don't know what you do in situations like that. I still have a hard time with that now. You never really get a chance to have closure, and that's very frustrating because it just hangs. I think it happens a lot because death just sneaks up on you. It's rarely planned. It seems that we have to find a way to be able to say goodbye.

I am handling a case now with a hospitalized woman and her daughter, and I feel very good about it. The daughter is giving me a lot of feedback. She thanks me for listening to her and says, "I love you and please have a good day tomorrow." I said to her, "If anything should happen to your mother I want to hear about it." She said, "I will not call you on your day off." So I just came right out and said to her, "Listen, I don't want to have to call the hospital." I know this is selfish of me and that this is my need, but that's what I mean by "be yourself!" You're only human and you have needs too. I was very honest with her, and I think she appreciated it because I care.

If there is somebody you don't like, and they die and you don't feel terrible, it's okay. It's okay to just be human and be who you are. In home care, you're not the boss. The patients and their families are running the show. You're not in a controlled environment, you're in their environment, and they call the shots. It's their right. You just fit in. Yet, it's hard not to feel you still represent the other side. The families and the patients often lump you in the same category as the doctors. Whether or not you are going to blur the line between "nurse" and "friend" is something that will change from case to case.

You don't go into these people's houses in a uniform, you go in your street clothes. You often become part of the family and when you do, it's a nice feeling. When I go see one elderly client, he looks forward to seeing me. If I go a day later than usual, he calls me and says, "Bonnie, are you coming this week?" When he sees me, he gives me a big hug and a kiss and asks, "Is your car parked in a good spot? Do you need a quarter to put in the meter?"

Home care is like an accident waiting to happen. The nature of our work is that the patient generally either dies or goes into a nursing home. So, you lose them no matter what and you have no choice but to accept it. Accept it and move on.

I've learned to give myself what I need. I shop at Saks Fifth Avenue, or I come home and relax, rent a movie and eat Chinese food. I have peers I can talk to now where I work. You need somebody in the same field that understands the frustrations. As caregivers, we must share our losses and gains, and support one another so that we can continue doing what we do best.

Part 3

Other
Dimensions
of Death

11

ALL OF YOUR LAUGHTER—ALL OF YOUR TEARS

By Debby Roth, M.S.C.

DEBBY ROTH *has been on staff at The Center for Help in Time of Loss as communications director and facilitator of the Healing through Humor support group. She is an ordained Interfaith minister and the author of* STEPPING STONES TO GRIEF RECOVERY.

There is nothing like facing your own death to show just how human you really are. Before it happened to me, I thought I had a fair handle on dying. After all, I'd worked at the center for more than five years, and I had certainly tried to look inside and confront my fears about death and loss. But when the report came back indicating that I had breast cancer, nothing was like I thought it would be. I was on the examining table when the doctor told me and I just stared at him. This wasn't supposed to be happening to me.

"Are you all right?" he asked. "I guess it's back to the drawing board," I said, realizing my concepts of "how it was" were no longer valid. I couldn't sort out the many feelings that were going on, but one of the strongest was a sense of failure, as if somehow I'd flunked life or done something wrong.

I think being a part of the center, surrounded by caregivers, gave me a special problem. I had a strong reluctance to assume the role of "helpee." I wanted to share my feelings, but I was furious at the slightest hint that I needed help because it made me feel like a lesser person, somehow weak and vulnerable. Any phrase like "I hear you" that smacked of the therapeutic method, made me absolutely crazy. These were my friends and they were also professionals and the two didn't seem to gel.

I became aware of the real value of having someone outside family and friends as a line of support. I felt the rise of that invisible barrier between the well and the sick, and I was outraged by it. As you may have already guessed, I was not easy to be around. I think it's fair to say that prior to this experience, I was not given to temper tantrums and was considered, if perhaps a bit stubborn, pretty easy to get along with. What the diagnosis of cancer did was remove the lid on my emotions. It was like being on a roller coaster and everything seemed exaggerated: normal impatience became childish rage, spontaneity and playfulness took on a tinge of hysteria. Fear can do that. I think my intensity scared everyone, including myself. I'm not sure that being in caregiving always makes us worse patients, but I suspect there is some correlation. Maybe it's that health care "managers" are particularly insulted to discover what way down deep they always knew: human beings are in control of very few things, and life and death are mysteries that cannot be handled by formulas and rules.

From my all too human perspective clouded by fear, I was given a new view of the world of health care and it appeared as distorted as Alice's wonderland. I was sitting in a radiology room of a large New York teaching hospital. I was being photographed so the radiologist could find the correct area to inject a blue dye that would mark the site of the biopsy for the surgeon. A routine mammography had picked up some suspicious cells and since there was no palpable tumor, the location had to be pinpointed by another method. The young woman who was attempting to get the right picture was pleasant, but harried. Above the machinery I spotted a poster on the wall that shouted: "BREAST CANCER, THE DREADED DISEASE!"

"Who put that up?" I asked.

"Oh, the hospital administration, I think," she said.

"That's pretty stupid," I told her.

"Yeah, but they want it there," she said.

At that exact moment the door opened and a middle-aged doctor entered accompanied by a young assistant. The older one had an accent that turned out to be Hungarian, but to me it immediately called up Auschwitz. I caught the last few words he was speaking to his student. "Ya, vasn't he a nice, benign man," he was saying.

"Benign, benign," I called out, "keep that thought in mind." The two doctors looked at me curiously, as if to say, "Did I hear a voice coming out of that body?"

Not allowing themselves to be distracted, the younger one asked, "How much dye will you inject?" Before his teacher could reply, I piped up.

"Yoo-hoo, do you see me? There's a person in here," I said pointing to the middle of my chest. Only the younger one looked up. "Oh, this is just technical stuff," he said,

"You wouldn't be interested." The procedure was painless, and the doctors were so pleased to have hit the right spot on the first try that I just retreated inside myself, until the younger man said, "You can go to Admitting now."

"I don't know where it is," I said. My voice quivered and suddenly he seemed to notice me. "Is something the matter?" he asked. "I'm scared," I said.

"Oh," he said. "I don't know where it is either, but I'll go with you." I felt a lump of tears in my throat at the first sign of recognition. We found our way up a back staircase, and he turned me over to an admitting nurse.

"You're late!" she barked. My young doctor friend looked as confused as I did. I could hear the White Rabbit, "You're late, you're late, for a very important date..."

Two weeks later, I was back in the same hospital coming out of anesthesia after a mastectomy. Somebody had his head very close to mine and his face was tight-lipped with rage. "I don't enjoy being called kid," he said. I must have insulted him while I was under.

"I'm sorry," I said, "I don't know what happened, but the anesthesia must be making me feel paranoid," I offered. "You don't just *feel* paranoid," he said, "You *are* paranoid."

The next thing I heard was a woman's voice, softly reprimanding me. "You're not behaving nicely at all," she said. "You're snapping at everyone."

I have no idea what I had been saying or doing, but as I came awake I was wary, and I made a firm decision after that to say as little as possible. As I waited over the next few days in the hospital to learn if the cancer had spread to the nodes, and if I would need chemotherapy or any further treatment, I came to a conclusion about whether or not I wanted to buck what seemed to me an indifferent and insensitive system. This is not to say that many nurses weren't kind, and in fact my own surgeon was particularly understanding and compassionate; characteristics not often attributed to his profession. One thing he told me was extremely calming. I had been wondering, as is often the case, what I had done physically or emotionally that might have caused the disease. The surgeon was just leaving my room when he turned back to face me. "If you learn one thing from me and one thing only," he said, "you didn't do anything wrong. So many patients feel guilty and guilt is a waste of time."

Of course, it's natural to want to find a cause so that you can feel there is a way to prevent a reoccurrence. Taking responsibility for your health can be useful, and anything that takes away the "victim mentality" seems to me to be helpful. But, and it's an important "but," guilt for the past can be just as harmful and imprisoning. All of this is to say that I saw much that was humane and caring in the medical field, but the pressure and bureaucracy in the hospital created an often inhuman atmosphere. My conclusion, however was to accept what I was not about to change. There was no way I could see to make a dent in the hospital system and my own choice would be to get out of there as soon as possible. It crossed my mind that maybe the hospital experience shouldn't be all that wonderful— what if it was such an appealing place that nobody wanted to leave? No, I'd settle for escape and leave the reform to others.

The pathology report was like a pardon from the governor. The nodes were all negative and there was no evidence of cancer anywhere—it had all come out in the mastectomy. There would be no chemotherapy. Although I would be considered high risk from now on, and under scrutiny, I experienced a wild sense of freedom. In fact, wildness seemed to dominate the months before and after the mastectomy.

If I was a little taken aback by my own behavior, I saw how it really troubled my family and friends. The child in me had emerged and would not be denied. The line between childlike and childish was blurred. I remember one of my closest friends becoming teary just before I went into the hospital.

"I just realized that I might lose you," she told me. "I could imagine you saying, 'take that trip we planned together—do it for both of us.'" My reaction was to go berserk. "Forget that scene," I shouted. "If I'm going to die, why don't you come with me!"

Another friend who had been endlessly patient with me finally threw up her hands when I refused to rest on my first day home, going directly to a class at the seminary where I was studying to become an Interfaith minister. I couldn't wait to show my fellow students and the teacher that I was alive and well. I remember one man coming up to my table at lunch after class and whispering in my ear, "You're a true warrior." And that was what was so puzzling. I think I was both courageous and outrageous—a warrior and a brat. As a matter of fact, later I was intrigued to learn from a Scottish friend, who is into mythology, that Amazon women used to cut off their right breasts in order to use a bow and arrow more efficiently for battle, and that the word "amazon" actually means "without breast." Although it seemed to be going a bit far, I must concede, I liked the comparison. I even speculated briefly on whether this whole experience wasn't some unconscious way for me to express my courage. It was certainly the first time I ever felt validated as a person who stood up under fire. All my other life battles like divorce, loneliness and aging were private ones that were rarely seen or acknowledged.

On the other hand, my impatience and my outbursts were startling. I was sure that such behavior was uncharacteristic and disappointing to those who felt they knew me better. "She's not herself," was, I think, the general conclusion. For sure I wasn't acting the way I usually did.

My six week recovery period was mostly wonderful. And at least a few things fell into place. For the first time that I can remember, I followed only my inner direction which was actually the advice of my doctor. "Rest when you are tired, eat when you are hungry. You're your own best guide." I seemed to need very little sleep, but when I was tired I went right off without a thought. I was obsessed by rearranging furniture, and adding plants and light to my room. I even went in search of an indoor fountain so that I could have the sense of being near water in a city apartment. Each new thing I added to the decor seemed to require a shift in the balance. A new ashtray made a lamp look out of place, a new pillow changed the color flow. What seemed like a simple diversion into decorating, gave me a new perspective on this human experience.

I felt in the deepest core of myself an urge toward integrity. I felt there was a rightness to all things, based on balance and wholeness. It seemed as if each of us had a canvas to work on representing our lives, on which we could attempt to keep that balance intact. I was aware that I had worked hard to form a self-image that would be pleasing to others and myself. Make nice, don't be selfish. If uncomfortable feelings intrude on the picture, cover them over. Maybe rework a piece over here and then balance it over there, but nothing too drastic.

Then suddenly a force intruded that would not yield to a cover-up. The threat of death precipitated that force. All hell seemed to break loose on my canvas and there was no way to integrate the old with what was happening. I used to think I'd rather die than act like a fool, or worse, appear unkind. I learned differently.

Actually, a few years ago I began to paint and went for some lessons. I remember my teacher telling me not to try working everything out on one canvas. Let yourself go on one, try a disciplined still-life on the other. He promised me if I kept at it the two would come together.

It's almost two years since my operation. I can't say that the whole "picture" has come together yet. My work with death and loss is focused primarily on a laughter group. Some of the same people who come to support group to express their grief also meet once a month for the purpose of laughing together. When you cry, your head empties and when you laugh, it usually starts you coughing and gets some heaviness off your chest. It's good to release some of the bottled-up energy and even better to come together and share. I had thought when I sat down to write this chapter that I would discuss the therapeutic value of laughter and tears. But methods of releasing emotions, though they are helpful, are only techniques. When you go to care for someone who is dying, or you are suddenly confronted with your own death, these techniques may even get in the way.

What I've begun to realize through being on the other side of the fence is that even when you think you're not imposing your beliefs on the patient, there are subtle expectations that all of us have. We want death to be "comfortable," and most of us admire dignity in the face of disaster. But that's not always possible. The important thing to realize is that individual balance and wholeness are unique to each person.

The places each of us mask all of our lives in order to cope may, if we're lucky, be uncovered under stress, allowing us to relate to life and death in a more genuine way. But the process of unmasking can be very uncomfortable for patient and caregiver alike. In the long run, I believe, at each given moment all of us are doing the best we can do.

I don't know that I will be any better prepared when death comes again. I am deeply grateful for the opportunity to start on a fresh canvas. I like to think that each of us is working on a separate piece of a larger work, and that when we do achieve a balance and a sense of integrity, our work can be joined to the larger whole. Of course, knowing my tendency to overwork things, I suspect I'll need someone to take the paint brushes away and say, "It's done."

12

BEYOND DEATH

By Emily LeVier, M.S.C.

EMILY LEVIER *is a founding member of The Center for Help in Time of Loss where she is support group coordinator and leader of the training programs for volunteers. She is an ordained Interfaith minister and was trained by Dr. Elisabeth Kübler-Ross' staff members. An associate member of the Foundation of Thanatology, she is currently studying at the Barbara Brennan School of Healing in East Hampton, New York.*

Working with terminal patients wasn't a choice for me. In fact, it wasn't anything I had even thought about. One day I was talking with Mary, the founder and director of the center, and she happened to mention that she needed someone to volunteer to help one of the cancer patients. It felt right for me to do this, so I volunteered. That was the beginning of a complete shift in my perspective about life and death.

I went over to meet Jackie, the patient, and we instantly formed a friendship. I considered myself a friend who was coming in to help out, not a caregiver. She wasn't threatened by my presence because I wasn't a nurse, and, at that time, not even a nurse's aide. She was in deep denial about her death at that point and would talk often about going back to work. I respected and supported her denial. As a result, a deep bond began to form between us which grew deeper over the next few months. She was a very proud and private woman who preferred doing things for herself. I never interfered until one day when she was struggling to get a gown over her head. I finally said, "Jackie, I'm here to help you." She stopped struggling and said, "All right! But you have to stand behind me and not look at my belly." The cancer had metastasized to her liver, which made her stomach very bloated and distorted. I agreed not to look, but trying to help her from behind wasn't working. I said, "Do you really think I would judge how you look?" She said, "No," and started to cry. Then she said something I would remember for as long as I was with her. She said, "This is the most humiliating thing that could ever happen to me—having someone dress me!" The tears were streaming down her cheeks. I cried with her and felt the deep humiliation that she was feeling.

Then she confided a very strange thing to me. She said, "I have always known that I was not going to die a quick death. I knew it would be a long drawn-out illness, and I knew there would be some very loving and kind woman to help me. All my life, every time I met a woman I wondered if she was the one who would help me die." We hugged and cried some more, and that seemed to be a turning point in her acceptance of her death. From that moment on, our relationship became one of total acceptance and unconditional love for one another.

We had many heart-to-heart talks about life and death. Once when we were talking, she asked me what I thought it was like in heaven. I said, "I don't know, but if you get there before I do maybe you can let me know." I was kidding, but she suddenly became very serious and stared at me for a long time. Then she said, "I will. If I can, I will let you know how it is there." I didn't think much about it at the time because there was so much to do.

Her humor and simplicity of personality were so pure. One night I was helping her from the bathroom back to her bed. We were swaying back and forth down the hall with our arms around each other, and I said, "You'd think we were dancing." She replied, "Aren't we?" She was like that. In the midst of painful acceptance, she could also see the funny predicament we humans are in.

She was a wonderful teacher. She would tell me what she needed me to do each day. Sometimes she would say, "Emily, don't talk today, just sit by my bed." Other times she would want me to read to her or hold her hand in silence. By this time she had hospice workers and nurses around the clock. She had asked the nurses to keep me on the case with her and they thought this was a good idea because of our relationship. They taught me to give shots for the pain because she was having trouble swallowing by this time. I was very nervous about doing this as it was the first time I had ever given a shot to anyone. Jackie helped me to ease my anxiety by saying, "You know you would never hurt me so don't worry, you'll be fine." She would tell me I gave better shots than the nurses. I'm sure that wasn't true, but it was her way of making me comfortable with the shots.

At this point, she began to withdraw more and more into the spirit world. I could almost see her come and go.

She would lie there in bed with her eyes closed for long periods of time. I would think she was sleeping, and suddenly she'd open her eyes and say something very profound that I couldn't understand at the time. For example, one day she opened her eyes, looked at me and said, "I was thinking about the circle, Emily." I said, "What circle, Jackie?" She said, "The circle of infinity." After Jackie's death, one day I was reading *A Course in Miracles* and when I started reading about the circle of infinity I was astonished. I knew Jackie had never heard of *A Course in Miracles*. But she certainly had experienced what this book was saying:

> Beyond the body, beyond the sun and stars, past everything you see and yet somehow familiar, is an arc of golden light that stretches as you look into a great and shining circle. And all the circle fills with light before your eyes. The edges of the circle disappear, and what is in it is no longer contained at all. The light expands and covers everything, extending to infinity forever shining and with no break or limit anywhere. Within it everything is joined in perfect continuity. Nor is it possible to imagine that anything could be outside, for there is nowhere that this light is not. *(Text, p. 417)*

I remember the last time I spoke to Jackie. She was propped up in bed with pillows and a nurse, Jeannie, was sitting on a small stool by her bed. Jackie tried to find the strength to smile when she saw me enter the room, but I motioned with my hand that she need not try. I could see the smile in her eyes. I reached for her hand. Jeannie instinctively got up and went into the kitchen for something.

I looked into Jackie's eyes and saw a peace that I hadn't seen before. I knew she was leaving her body soon to go to that place that we had talked about so many times.

It seemed as if she were already there and yet, still here at the same time. I said, "I'm not sad, you know, because I think where you are going is beautiful." She tried to nod her head and whispered, "There is nothing to be afraid of." Then, as if on cue, Jeannie entered the room again. I kissed Jackie on the forehead and said, "I'll see you again." she whispered, "Thank you!"

That was the last time I saw her, but not the last of our relationship. I felt a peace within me as I was driving home. The call came about an hour after I arrived home. Jackie had made her transition. The normal confusion of the dinner hour at home had begun, and the living continued unaware that a most evolved and beautiful soul had just departed this earthly plane.

A week later, I was riding in my car and the words to a long forgotten hymn came floating into my mind:

Blest be the ties that bind
our hearts in Christian love.
The fellowship of kindred minds
is like to that above.

Suddenly, I knew in my heart that this was Jackie's message to me. She was telling me how it was there. I stopped the car and cried with joy and sadness. How I missed her! That was the first communication from her. The next communication preceded a series of events that turned my life upside down.

My son, Raymond, was in the burn unit of Westchester Medical Center in Valhalla, New York. He was suffering from third-degree burns on sixty-five percent of his body and the doctors had told me he would not survive. I was sitting in the waiting room when I suddenly remembered that Jackie had come to me the night of the fire. I had turned off the light to go to sleep and, as I closed my eyes, I saw Jackie's face as clear as if she were standing there. I wasn't dreaming. I hadn't fallen asleep yet. She stared at me the way she did the last time I saw her and said, "There is nothing to be afraid of." It hit me like a bolt of lightning! My God! I thought to myself, she knew! She knew about the fire and she came to tell me not to be afraid. I sat stunned for a while, then I heard the nurse saying, "You can go in now, Mrs. LeVier, your son wants to see you." Jackie was right! There was nothing to be afraid of. My son lived.

I feel her presence with me at times even now. Each spring, when the tiger lilies bloom, I think of her. She used to love the tiger lilies. They are blooming now as I write this chapter and I have no doubt that she knows I am writing about her.

After Jackie's death, my next two experiences with dying patients confirmed for me that there is so much more beyond the scope of my limited perception.

Gertrude was an older woman in her seventies who was dying of cancer. Her husband, Frank, was her primary care person. By this time, I had founded Helping Hands, a small group of nurse's aides who had been trained by the center to work with terminal patients. I had been called because Frank needed to get some sleep at night. He was caring for Gert around the clock. Frank and I would sit at the kitchen table while Gert was resting, and he would tell me long stories about their life together. They didn't have children, so it was always Frank and Gert sharing everything together.

Once, when we were talking, he told me about his near-death experience and how it changed his beliefs. He said he had died on the operating table and was brought back. He also said he had no fear of death now because he knew what it was like, and he knew that life continues. I was very curious and wanted to hear all about his experience in detail. He said, "You go through something like a tunnel, but you know there is a light that you're going towards, and there are people there to show you where to go when you reach the light." He wasn't afraid of Gert dying, he said, because he knew where she was going, but he was afraid to have to live his life here without her. Then he added, "But I know we will be together again."

I was supposed to be on duty Friday evening, but Frank called that morning and said that he didn't need me because Gert had slept the night before and he felt rested. I told him I would be in the neighborhood that afternoon and I would stop in for a visit. When I arrived there, Frank told me that Gert had asked him when her sisters were coming to visit again and he told her, "Tomorrow is Saturday, they will be here in the morning." Gert replied, "Well, they'll be too late." I told Frank that I thought I should stay with him because Gert knew something we didn't know.

I stayed with him and about two hours later Gert asked to have the minister come. She also asked to see the next door neighbors whom she was very close to. I am always amazed by the greater plan that takes place at the time of someone's death. Like clockwork, the minister came, the neighbors came, and Frank went back into the kitchen to eat while I sat with Gert.

She looked at me and said, "Shrouds have no pockets, you know." Her breathing began to change from slow long breaths to shorter rasping breaths, which is always a sign that the dying process has begun. I called Frank into the living room where Gert was in her hospital bed, and he sat by her holding her hand and talking gently to her while I sat at her feet looking on. His conversation went like this:

> Gert, it has always been Frank and Gert, and we have always done everything together, so we're going to do this together, too. Just take your time. There's no need to rush because we have plenty of time. Don't be afraid. I'm going with you as far as I can go. Gert, now we're going to go through a long tunnel and there will be people in front of you and people behind you, but there's no need to hurry, we're all going to the light. Now, look to the light. It almost seems blinding as you get closer to it, but don't be afraid. Just keep heading toward the light. This is as far as I can go with you, but there will be someone there to tell you where to go. I'll be along soon.

Gert breathed her last breath and it was over. I sat there astonished at what I had just witnessed. He actually took her through the tunnel to the world beyond. Frank began to sob and I left them alone. I went into the kitchen to make the necessary calls for him. I will never forget this very humble man who taught me about the journey from this world to the next.

Lorie was a beautiful young woman who was diagnosed with cancer shortly after she had gotten her degree in family counseling. It was the kind of cancer that spreads rapidly. She struggled intensely with having to let go of her two young daughters. We had many intimate talks about the process of letting go. I had just come through a deep loss of my own and Lorie would make me sit by her bed so she could counsel me. Before she died, she told me I had given her something no one else could give her. I said, "What, Lorie?" She said, "You let me do the thing I do best —counseling! You didn't take that away from me."

At the moment of Lorie's death, I was standing at the foot of her bed. I felt her spirit go through my body and felt a bubble surround me. For two days, I was immersed in a peace so complete that the only way I can describe what I felt would be to say it was "the peace of God that passeth understanding." I knew this was Lorie's gift to me. We had shared a lot of pain together and now she was sharing her peace with me. I am grateful to her for the experience of knowing that peace is not an outward condition, but an inner state of being.

This may not seem unusual to caregivers who have had these experiences with dying patients, but I wonder why we don't share more about the continuity of life being a reality. These experiences led me to a deeper inner questioning about life and death. Questions like: What am I beyond the body? Can we really communicate with our loved ones who have died? This last question has been answered many times in my experience as a support group coordinator. From time to time, someone will approach me very shyly asking if they can speak to me privately. They generally start by saying, "Please don't think I'm crazy, but..." Then they share with me some very meaningful experience they have had connecting with their dead loved one.

Tony, a young man in my support group, shared an experience he had with his father shortly after his father's death. He had a dream about his father, and in the dream his father told him there were five paint cans in the basement by the boiler that were flammable and to remove the cans from the basement. He hadn't told anyone of this experience. I asked him if he'd known the paint cans were in the basement before the dream. He said, "No. I had no idea the paint cans were there. The next day I went down into the basement, and sure enough, there they were. Just like he said in the dream. I took them out and threw them away." I said, "Then it must be true." It gave him great comfort to know that his father really could communicate with him. Since then, he has had other experiences which he has shared with me and he no longer doubts that these are true experiences of communication with his father.

Julie is a widow whose husband died three years ago. She is a very successful businesswoman who runs her own company. This is Julie's account to me of how she experienced her husband's presence:

> Every time I'm at the point where I can't go on anymore some thing happens. The first time it happened, I was crying hysterically in my bedroom. I was crying and saying, "How could you leave me?" I was very despairing. All of a sudden, this glowing form came into the room. It's hard to explain it. It's not like any ghost you have ever seen on television. It was silver in color and it glowed. It swirled around and it came right to me, and I knew it was him. He laid down next to me in bed and it felt as if I absorbed him into my body. I suddenly had such peace. I can't begin to tell you how it felt. I stopped crying. I stopped feeling bad. I just felt so much peace. I was the happiest that I've ever been, and I said, "Oh thank you," and then I fell asleep. It happened about five times. Each time the liquid form would come. It always happened when I was at my lowest point. I think the interesting part is that I could never make it happen. Many nights I would say, "Please come, I need you now," but I could not will it to happen. Some people may say this is crazy, but I know this is real and it has given me such peace and comfort. I know by the way I feel afterward.

Rosanne is a young widow whose husband died ten months ago. She is a registered nurse; a very mentally healthy person with an exceptionally positive outlook on life. This is her account of what happened to her:

There have been many instances since Bill died when I knew he was with me helping me to get through this, but there are certain ones that stand out in my mind more than others. Recently, I had a birthday that I didn't want to acknowledge, so I worked that day. Just before I was ready to go home, long-stemmed roses came for me at the office. Bill used to send me roses for my birthday. For a second, I thought they were from him. They were from his mother. I felt kind of strange and it took me awhile before I could call her to thank her. When I called her, she was at work and had to go to another phone to talk. I could feel her on the phone. She was shaking and crying, and she said, "Rosanne, last night I had a dream about Bill. I haven't dreamed about him since he died. When I went to bed, he came to me in a dream and said, 'Mom, tomorrow is Rosanne's birthday, don't forget it. Send her a dozen red roses.'" She said she woke up and sat straight up in bed, and she knew it was Bill speaking to her telling her to send roses.

The other incident was with the song "Day-O." We liked that song. For a while, every place I would go I would hear that song. People would just start singing it in front of me. It was driving me crazy. I knew it meant something, but I didn't know what. A friend of mine said to me, "Why don't you just stop trying to figure it out and see what happens." So, I forgot about it. Before Bill died, we were talking about getting a kitten and we never did. Bill loved cats and they loved him. I was at a friend's house one night when her daughter Tammy came in with a beautiful little kitten. As soon as I saw the kitten I knew I was supposed to have him. I asked Tammy what his name was and she said he didn't have a name. Then it hit me! Of course! His name is Day-O. I knew it was a gift from Bill. Sometimes, when these things happen, I think maybe I'm really going crazy from the grief. And yet, there is another part of me that knows it's true, and I always feel very peaceful and happy afterwards. How could it be crazy? It's hard to explain to anyone, but I know how I feel and you can only know by the way you feel. If anyone had told me this a year ago, I, too, would have said they were crazy, but something has happened inside of me. I know I can communicate with Bill. His body may not be here, but his essence is still very much alive. I can feel him touching my heart and I know he lives, wherever he is. I also know Bill would have wanted people to know this because he believed in life after death.

So often, people are told by well-meaning friends that they must let go of the person who died and get on with their lives. I like to rephrase this by saying, "Letting go means letting go of your attachment and your need for them. You don't have to put them out of your heart to get on with your life." When someone approaches me with an experience now, I always respond by saying, "Love does not die—trust your own heart."

AFTERWORD

By Patricia McVeigh, M.S.W., A.C.S.W.

PATRICIA MCVEIGH *is on staff at The Center for Help in Time of Loss. She is a psychotherapist who works with people with AIDS and those in grief. She facilitates the Cancer Survivors Support Group and has extensive experience in the field of death and dying in hospitals and private practice.*

Those of us working with individuals facing death are called upon to journey with them no matter where that journey takes them or us. This is by no means an easy journey to take, but it is one that we must take if we are to remain true to our patients and ourselves.

Embarking on such a journey implies that we are wholly involved in our patient and that we do not impose our expectations, values or beliefs onto them. It can be a painful journey at times and, in order to do this, we, as caregivers, must be able to be open and honest about ourselves. An important area that we must look closely at is our own personal experience with loss.

We have all had losses in our lives, for losses are a part of life. Exploring and grieving our losses involves getting acquainted with many feelings that are often overwhelming in their intensity. Such feelings often include fear, anger, despair, helplessness, hopelessness, and guilt.

Unless we are in touch with our own pain, I am not certain that we can truly hear the pain that others are experiencing. We run the risk of bringing our own issues into the journey and sometimes this takes the form of running away psychologically from our patient.

To be with someone in the midst of their anger, despair or hopelessness, we need to be able to identify our own feelings, particularly the ones we're not so comfortable with. We need to acknowledge the full range of our feelings and learn to accept them for what they are: an important part of us that makes us fully human, a total being. If we can accept such feelings as rage, anger, guilt, and despair within ourselves, then we can accept them in another person and accompany them on what is perhaps the most intimate journey of their lives.

I consider it an honor when I am invited to share in a patient's journey towards death. What my patients have taught me is how significant life is and how significant relationships are. I've learned that we often have only brief moments with people. Life comes and goes so quickly, so I attempt to make the moments of my encounter count by dropping the games and masks that separate us from one another. The vehicle that gets the two of us together is often the illness, but that's not why we're there with each other. We're there to share something together. It is the relationship that ultimately is significant, the human experience of journeying together.

So the question is: How can we stay in this very difficult field day after day, year after year, when so much of what surrounds us is death? How can we remain human in the face of death? This is a difficult question to answer, but it's one that we must each answer for ourselves. I firmly believe that we can spend a lifetime in the field and still remain human in the face of death, but in order to do so we must be aware of the question and our own personal answer.

BLEST ARE THE SORROWING:
THEY SHALL BE CONSOLED

And what does it mean to mourn?
I asked the multitude.
And an old man stepped forward.

To mourn, he said, is to be given a second heart.
It is to care so deeply
that you show your ache in person.

To mourn is to be unashamed of tears.
It is to be healed
and broken
and built-up
all in the same moment.

Blessed are you if you can minister to others
with a heart that feels
with a heart that hurts
with a heart that loves
and blessed are you if you can minister to others
with a heart that serves
and a heart that sees the need before it's spoken.

To mourn is to forget yourself for a moment and get lost
in someone else's pain
and then,
to find yourself
in the very act of getting lost.

To mourn is to be an expert
in the miracle
of being careful with another's pain.

It is to be full of the willingness
of forever reaching out to
and picking up
and holding carefully
those who hurt.

To mourn is to sing with the dying
and to be healed
by the song
and the death.

—AUTHOR UNKNOWN

Part 4

The
Caregiver's
Workbook

THE CAREGIVER'S WORKBOOK

The following workbook section is adapted from the center's training program.*

We suggest that you take one hour or more each week of quiet time to respond to the questions. We also suggest you write your responses in a notebook, or in this book in the spaces provided, in order to measure your progress. Each exercise involves a series of questions. You may want to answer them individually or you may want to read them all and then write for several minutes about the various issues they bring up. Another possibility is to simply discuss the questions with a fellow caregiver. The ideal situation would be to discuss the material in a peer support group that meets regularly.

*Portions of this section were originally published by The Center for Help in Time of Loss under the title, "How to Handle the Needs of the Terminally Ill at Home," Copyright, 1982 by Lois Lorenz.

Some of the exercises also involve assignments where you must take an action. If you are using this workbook in a peer group, you will want to carry out the assignment during the week and discuss it the next time you meet.

While we have offered some guidelines for working with terminal patients and their families, we also recognize the value of your own life experiences in preparing you for this work. This workbook is meant to tap these experiences, helping you to know yourself a little better and, in a sense, to become your own teacher.

■ EXERCISE I

Goal: To understand typical feelings people experience
when helping or being helped.

Thinking/Writing

1. When you think about helping other people, what does
this mean to you?

_____

_____

_____

_____

_____

_____

2. How do you expect to feel giving help?

_____

_____

_____

_____

_____

3. Is it easier for you to give help or to receive it?

_____

_____

_____

_____

_____

4. How do you feel when others ask you for help or for a favor?

_____

_____

_____

_____

_____

_____

5. If serious illness or trouble were to come to someone in your home, what reaction would you expect from people you know?

_____

_____

_____

_____

_____

_____

6. Would you be able to ask for help? From whom?

_____

_____

_____

_____

_____

_____

7. Do other family members share your views?

_____

_____

_____

_____

Assignment

We often take on more than is reasonable or feels "right" for us in both our work and personal life. Choose someone you could ask to help you — at home or at work — to make your life a little easier. Once you have decided on this person, ask him or her for some help. After you have done this, ask yourself:

1. What resistance was there in yourself to doing it? Did you put it off or feel uneasy about it?

_____

_____

_____

_____

_____

_____

_____

_____

2. How can you give yourself permission to do it a little more easily next time?

_____

_____

_____

_____

_____

_____

_____

_____

■ EXERCISE II

Goal: To understand appropriate limits in giving help.

<u>Thinking/Writing</u>

In the last exercise we worked with the concepts of giving and receiving help. In this exercise we ask you to think about when you need to set limits on how much you can give. The following questions may help you to focus your thoughts and experiences.

1. Are there certain people towards whom you feel more naturally giving than others?

_____

_____

_____

_____

2. What is it like for you to give of yourself to these people?

_____

_____

_____

_____

3. How is it different with the people towards whom you feel less giving?

_____

_____

_____

_____

4. Have you ever said "no" to someone who asked a favor?

_____

5. What was this like for you?

_____

_____

_____

_____

_____

6. If you have never said "no," what do you think it would be like?

_____

_____

_____

_____

Assignment

Thinking about your life at home or at work, is there a situation in which you should say "no" to someone or set limits on what you can reasonably do? Make a plan for how you can accomplish this and try it out. Look at any thoughts or feelings that get in your way. How did you feel afterwards?

_____

_____

_____

_____

_____

_____

▪ EXERCISE III

Goal: To explore your comfort level when talking about the issues surrounding death.

Thinking/Writing

In this exercise we ask you to consider your own feelings about discussing death or illness. The following questions may help you in exploring your personal views and comfort zones.

1. Who are the people in your life now with whom you can talk about death, or loss, or important issues?

_____

_____

_____

_____

2. With whom can't you talk about these issues?

_____

_____

_____

_____

3. How comfortable do you feel talking about death or illness?

_____

_____

_____

_____

4. Are there times or situations that make it easier to talk about death?

_____

_____

_____

_____

5. Are there times or situations that make it hard to talk about death?

_____

_____

_____

_____

6. What questions, if any, would you rather not be asked about dying?

_____

_____

_____

_____

Assignment

Think about the situations in your family life and at work when someone in your family or work environment was embarrassed or uncomfortable talking about dying. Think about the situations in which *you* may have been uncomfortable. How might you handle this situation when it arises again? Do an experiment for yourself to test your comfort zone. The next time you meet someone socially and they ask what you do, talk about your profession as a health care worker in the field of death and dying. Write about their reactions, and about *your reaction* to their reactions.

_____

_____

_____

_____

_____

_____

_____

_____

_____

_____

_____

_____

_____

_____

_____

_____

_____

_____

_____

_____

_____

_____

_____

_____

■ EXERCISE IV

Goal: To explore your feelings about death and loss in your
　　　own life.

Thinking/Writing

When someone close to you dies, it is very common to feel
not only loss but also regret for those things you didn't do
or say, that you felt you should have. Choose a person in
your life that you are very close to and answer the following questions:

1. If this person were to die today, what regrets would you
　 have about the things you didn't do or say?

_____

_____

_____

_____

_____

2. What regrets would you have about things this other
　 person did not have a chance to do?

_____

_____

_____

_____

_____

3. What regrets would you have about your relationship?

_____

_____

_____

_____

_____

_____

5. Make a list of changes that you could make in your life
   right now to avoid having regrets.

_____

_____

_____

_____

_____

_____

_____

_____

Assignment

Act on one of the changes you listed. How did it feel?

_____

_____

_____

_____

_____

_____

_____

_____

■ EXERCISE V

Goal: To recognize how memories can help in the healing
process during bereavement.

1. Select a picture of someone you have cared about who
has died and, looking at the picture, write down your
memories about this person. Remember, memories can
be both good and not-so-good.

\
\
\
\
\
\
\
\

2. Which memories were easiest to write about?

\
\
\
\
\

3. Which memories were more difficult to write about?

\
\
\
\

■ EXERCISE VI

Goal: To find ways that will ease the initial introduction to
      patient and family.

Part A

1. How do you usually feel when meeting someone new?

_____

_____

_____

_____

2. What would you want to know about a family before
visiting them?

_____

_____

_____

_____

3. How might you introduce yourself to a family you were
meeting for the first time?

_____

_____

_____

_____

4. How would you expect a family to react to a first visit?

_____

_____

_____

_____

5. What do you expect to be easiest for you about the first visit?

_____

_____

_____

_____

6. What do you expect to be hardest for you about the first visit?

_____

_____

_____

_____

Part B

If you were faced with the following situations on your first visit to a family, how would you respond? Write down your response to each situation. What feelings would be set off in you personally?

1. Your patient, an 83-year-old man with lung cancer and a prognosis of a few weeks to live, talks to you about wanting to take his own life rather than continue an existence which to him has become useless.

_____

_____

_____

_____

_____

_____

2. You arrive at your patient's home. Her condition is very poor. Her husband takes you into another room and begins to cry as he tells you how he doesn't know what he will do when his wife dies.

_____

_____

_____

_____

_____

3. Your patient, a 63-year-old man, orders you to get him his lunch, not to forget his medication, arrange the sheets on his bed, and change the television channel — right now!

_____

_____

_____

_____

_____

Which would be the easiest situation for you to deal with? Why?

_____

_____

_____

Which would be the most difficult? Why?

_____

_____

_____

■ EXERCISE VII

Goal: To think about a case situation and how you might
    be able to help if you were assigned to the family.

You have been asked to visit the Wagner family.

Joe and Barbara Wagner live together with their three
children in New Jersey. Joe has a middle-management
position in a large company. Barbara has her nursing
degree, but has not worked since her first child was born.
Since then she has remained home to raise the children. She
enjoys being a wife and mother, and is active in her church
and community affairs. Although Joe goes away for short
business trips several times a month, he and Barbara have
a caring relationship and feel they have a "good marriage."

All three children attend school. Robert is a serious student and plans to study law. Ginny has had some academic
problems, but has many friends and seems to value social
activities more. Maryann, the "baby" of the family, is
slightly immature for her age, but seems to be making a
fairly good adjustment to school and to her peer group.

Joe's parents live an hour away. They lead a separate and
somewhat isolated life, though relations between the gen-
erations are generally cordial, if not overtly close and
affectionate. Barbara's family lives in California where she
was raised, and where she and Joe attended school. She
moved to New Jersey when she and Joe were married and
considers New Jersey her home.

Joe was diagnosed with colon cancer nine months ago. He
has had surgery to attempt to remove the tumor, and is now
receiving a course of chemotherapy. The treatments are
given approximately every three weeks in his doctor's

office. He feels nauseous for several days after the treatment but wants to continue taking it.

Answer the following questions about the Wagner case.

1. What specific problems and concerns do you think each member of the family may have?

_____

_____

_____

_____

_____

_____

_____

_____

_____

_____

2. What specific kinds of help might they need at this time?

_____

_____

_____

_____

_____

_____

_____

_____

_____

_____

_____

3. What specific kinds of help might they need three
   months from now?

_____

_____

_____

_____

_____

_____

_____

4. How might you, as a caregiver, be helpful to them?

_____

_____

_____

_____

_____

_____

_____

5. What other services might be helpful to them?

_____

_____

_____

_____

_____

_____

_____

■ EXERCISE VIII

Goal: To help you assess and plan for your personal support and renewal system.

In this exercise we are asking you to take special time with your assignment. While past assignments have focused on helping you to look at past and present experiences and feelings in your life, this assignment helps you to plan for the future.

You may be asked by friends or even family, "How can you do this kind of work? Isn't it depressing?" By now we hope you have thought about the first part of this question and would like to help you consider the second. Working with others experiencing the immediacy of death and loss can be both extraordinarily gratifying and satisfying. It does, however, require us each to maintain a certain balance and objectivity in our lives. As with any sustained effort to help others, we may begin to feel drained if we lose a perspective on how our caring and giving needs to be equalized by being cared for and given to ourselves. This input into our lives may take many forms: it may come directly from other people as well as from the enthusiasm and excitement we receive from reading a new novel, cooking a gourmet meal (or dining out at a fine restaurant), or spending time alone in quiet meditation. What is rejuvenating and revitalizing to each of us will be unique and individual, but also quite crucial to our ability to maintain a balance in our everyday lives.

In this exercise we would like you to assess your support system, your emotional "credits and debits," what is given to you and what you give out. On the following pages, make a careful and thoughtful list, first of all your "expenditures" - to whom and to what you give your time and energy. Do not limit yourself to people, but include all the organizations, events, and responsibilities which claim your time and attention.

On the second page, with the same thoroughness, list your resources for emotional support and renewal. Use extra sheets if necessary.

When you have completed this part of the assignment, it is time for Part II. Make a final list of those areas in your life from which, with little additional effort, you could get support, but have not yet tapped. Be creative—you may find an unexpected wealth of resources you have overlooked.

SUPPORT AND RENEWAL CHECKLIST I

I give energy & support to...

_____
_____
_____
_____
_____
_____
_____
_____
_____
_____
_____
_____
_____

I receive energy & support from...

_____

_____

_____

_____

_____

_____

_____

_____

_____

_____

_____

_____

_____

SUPPORT AND RENEWAL CHECKLIST II
Untapped Resources

I could also receive energy and support from...

_____

_____

_____

_____

_____

_____

_____

_____

_____

_____

_____

_____

_____

■ EXERCISE IX

Goal: Finding resources for the patient and the family
   while creating a closure for yourself.

Often caregivers do not consider the importance of closure
with a family that their lives have become an integral part
of for many weeks. We hope to give you some ideas in this
exercise to create a closure for yourself and for the family.

1. Do you have a personal resource list?

_____

2. Have you done your own research to see what else may
   be available in the community?

_____

3. Do you have an information packet of community
   bereavement resources for the family?

_____

4. Does your job include follow-up service?

_____

If you have answered "no" to the above questions, put
together a resource list by doing some research to see what
is available in the community. Hospice programs, social
workers, clergy, bereavement groups in churches, friends,
or co-workers are good sources of information. Are there
ways you could pool your resources or work together to
develop a guide or information packet you could use?

Think about other ways that you can create a closure for yourself. You may come up with some ideas that we have not listed here. Maybe you want to receive some feedback from the family, or maybe you just want to express your own feelings to them about your experience caring for their loved one.

BIBLIOGRAPHY

■ Nursing/Caregiving

Banister, Olive K., and Jean A. Bobos. "Personal Communication." *Nursing Consultant*, The American Cancer Society, July 10, 1978.

Blondis, M. N. and B. E. Jackson. *Nonverbal Communication with Patients*. New York: John Wiley, 1977.

Epstein, C. *Nursing the Dying Patient: Learning Processes for Interaction*. Reston, Va: Reston Publishing, 1975.

Garfield, C. A., ed. *Psychosocial Aspects of Terminal Patient Care*. New York: McGraw-Hill, 1978.

Janken, Janice K. "The Nurse in Crisis." *Nursing Clinics of North America* 9, no. 1 (March 1974): 17-26.

Knapp, M. *Non-Verbal Communication in Human Interaction.* New York: Holt, Rinehart and Winston, 1972.

Long, L. and P. Prophit. *Understanding/Responding - A Communication Manual for Nurses.* Monterey, Calif: Wadsworth, 1981.

Mayerson, E. W. *Putting the Ill at Ease.* New York: Harper and Row, 1976.

Moffatt, B., et. al. *AIDS: A Self-Care Manual.* Santa Monica, Calif: IBS Press, 1987.

Montagu, Ashley. *Touching: The Human Significance of Skin.* New York: Harper & Row, 1971.

"Nurse-Client Communication: The Mutual Search for Meaning." In *Psychiatric Nursing.* Menlo Park, Calif: Addison Wesley Publishing, 1983.

Okun, B. F. *Effective Helping: Interviewing and Counseling Techniques.* North Scituate, Mass: Duxbury Press, 1976.

Pluckhan, M. *Human Communication: the Matrix of Nursing.* New York: McGraw Hill, 1978.

Prichard, E. R., et al., eds. *Social Work with the Dying Patient and Family.* New York: Columbia University Press, 1977.

Saunders, C., ed. *The Management of Terminal Disease.* London: Edward Arnold Publishers, 1978.

Schroeder, C. M. "Communicating with Hard-to-reach Patients." *Health and Social Work* 5 (February 1980): 35-39.

Shubin, S. "The Professional Hazard You Face in Nursing." *Nursing* 8, no. 7 (July 1978): 22-27.

■ Stress/Burnout

Cooper, C. L. and J. Marshal, eds. *White Collar and Professional Stress.* New York: John Wiley and Sons, 1980.

Freudenberger, Herbert J. "The Staff Burnout Syndrome in Alternative Institutions." *Psychotherapy: Theory, Research and Practice* 12, no. 1 (Spring 1975): 73-82.

Friel, M. and C. B. Tehan. "Counteracting Burn-out for the Hospice Caregiver." *Cancer Nursing* 3 (August 1980): 285-293.

Holmes, T. H. and R. H. Rahe. "The Social Readjustment Rating Scale." *Journal of Psychosomatic Research* 11, no. 1 (June 1967): 213-218.

McLean, A., ed. *Occupational Stress.* Springfield, Ill: Charles C. Thomas, 1974.

Monat, A., and R. S. Lazarus, eds. *Stress and Coping: An Anthology.* New York: Columbia University Press, 1977.

Pines, A. and C. Maslach. "Characteristics of Staff Burnout in Mental Health Settings." *Hospital and Community Psychiatry* 29, no. 4 (April 1978): 233-237.

Seyle, H. *Stress Without Distress.* Philadelphia: J. B. Lippincott, 1974.

■ Death/Dying

Kastenbaum, R. J. *Death, Society and Human Experience.* Saint Louis: C. V. Mosby, 1977.

Krant, M. J. *Death and Dignity: The Meaning and Control of Personal Death.* Springfield, Ill: Charles C. Thomas, 1974.

Kubler-Ross, E. *On Death and Dying.* New York: MacMillan Publishing, 1969.

Maguire, D. C. *Death by Choice.* New York: Doubleday and Company, 1974.

Moffatt, B. *Gifts for the Living: Conversations with Caregivers on Death and Dying.* Santa Monica, Calif: IBS Press, 1988.

Oden, T. C. *Should Treatment be Terminated? Moral Guidelines for Christian Families and Pastors.* New York: Harper and Row, 1976.

Ogg, E. "The Right to Die with Dignity." *Public Affairs Pamphlet no.587A.* New York: The Public Affairs Committee, 1983.

Parrish-Harra, C. *The New Age Handbook on Death and Dying.* Santa Monica, Calif: IBS Press, 1989.

Pattison, E. M. *The Experience of Dying.* Englewood Cliffs, N.J.: Prentice Hall, 1977.

Pincus, L. *Death and the Family.* New York: Pantheon Books, 1974.

Robinson, R. *Survivors of Suicide.* Santa Monica, Calif: IBS Press, 1989.

Schoenberg, B. et al., eds. *Psychosocial Aspects of Terminal Care.* New York: Columbia University Press, 1973.

Steinfels, P., and R. M. Veatch, eds. *Death Inside Out: The Hastings Center Report.* New York: Harper and Row, 1974.

Veatch, R. M. *Death, Dying and the Biological Revolution.* New Haven: Yale University Press, 1976.

■ Hospice

Buckingham, R. W. *The Complete Hospice Guide.* New York: Harper & Row, 1983.

Corr, C. A., and D. M. Corr, eds. "Hospice Care; Principles and Practice." *The Springer Series on Death and Suicide* Vol. 5. New York: Springer Publishing, 1983.

Friel, M. and C.B. Tehan. "Counteracting Burn-out for the Hospice Caregiver." *Cancer Nursing* 3 (August 1980): 285-293.

Lack, Sylvia. "Characteristics of a Hospice Program of Care." In *The Hospice: Development and Administration*, edited by Glen W. Davidson. Washington: Hemisphere Publishing, 1978.

Lusk, M. W. "The Psychosocial Evaluation of the Hospice Patient." *Social Work in Health Care* 8 (1983): 210-218.

Prichard, E. R., et al., eds. *Home Care: Living with Dying.* New York: Columbia University Press, 1979.

Saunders, C., D. H. Summers, and N. Teller, eds. *Hospice: The Living Idea.* Philadelphia: W. B. Saunders, 1981.

Zimmerman, J. M. *Hospice: Complete Care for the Terminally Ill.* Baltimore: Urban and Schwarzenberg, 1981.

■ Grief Recovery

Bowlby, John. *Loss: Sadness & Depression*, Vol. 3 of Attachment & Loss series. Basic Books, 1980.

Engel, G. "Grief and Grieving." In *A Sociological Framework for Patient Care*, edited by J. Folta and E. Deck. New York: John Wiley and Sons, 1966.

Freeman, L. *The Sorrow and the Fury: Overcoming Hurt and Loss From Childhood to Old Age.* Englewood Cliffs, N.J.: Prentice-Hall, 1978.

Glick, I. O., et al. *The First Year of Bereavement.* New York: John Wiley and Sons, 1974.

Hollingsworth, C. E., and R. O. Pasnau, eds. *The Family in Mourning: A Guide for Health Professionals.* New York: Grune and Stratton, 1977.

Marris, P. *Loss and Change.* New York: Random House, 1974.

Moffatt, B. *When Someone You Love Has AIDS: A Book of Hope for Family and Friends.* New York: NAL Penguin, 1987.

Parkes, C. M. *Bereavement: Studies of Grief in Adult Life.* New York: International Universities Press, 1973.

Parkes, C. M. "The First Year of Bereavement: A Longitudinal Study of the Reaction of London Widows to the Deaths of Their Husbands." *Psychiatry* 33, no. 4 (November 1970): 444-467.

Roth, D. *Stepping Stones to Grief Recovery.* Santa Monica, Calif: IBS Press, 1988.

Schoenberg, B., et al., eds. *Anticipatory Grief.* New York: Columbia University Press, 1974.

Schoenberg, B., et al., eds. *Bereavement: Its Psychosocial Aspects.* New York: Columbia University Press, 1975.

Schoenberg, B., et al., eds. *Loss and Grief: Psychological Management in Medical Practice.* New York: Columbia University Press, 1970.

Silverman, P. "The Widow to Widow Program." *Mental Hygiene* 53, no. 3 (July 1969): 333-337.

Silverman, P. "Widowhood and Preventive Intervention." *Family Coordinator* 21, no.1 (January 1972): 95-10.

Spiegel, Y. *The Grief Process: Anaylsis and Counseling.* Nashville: Abingdon Press, 1977.

■ Cancer - Caregiving

Abrams, Ruth D. *Not alone with Cancer. A Guide for Those Who Care: What to Expect; What to do.* Springfield, Ill: Charles C. Thomas, 1974.

Aker, Saundra, Gail Tilmont, and Vangee Harrison. *A Guide to Good Nutrition During and After Chemotherapy and Radiation*. Seattle: Fred Hutchinson Cancer Research Center, 1976.

Banister, Olive K., and Jean A. Bobos. "At-Home Rehab for Cancer Patients." *American Rehabilitation* 2, no. 3 (January-February 1977): 20-22.

Banister, Olive K., and Jean A. Bobos. "A Visiting Nurse Specializes in Cancer." *American Journal of Nursing* 70, no. 8 (August 1970): 1680-83.

Cancer Care, Inc. of the National Cancer Foundation. *The Impact, Costs, and Consequences of Catastrophic Illness on Patients and Families*. New York: Cancer Care, Inc. of the National Cancer Foundation, March 1973.

Christ, G. H. "A Psychosocial Assessment Framework for Cancer Patients and their Families." *Health and Social Work* 8 (Winter 1983): 57-64.

Kane, Rosalie A. "Communications in the Treatment of Cancer." *American Journal of Nursing* (May 1971): 944-48.

Lack, Sylvia. "The Hospice Concept - The Adult with Advanced Cancer." In *Proceedings of the American Cancer Society Second National Conference on Human Values & Cancer*. New York: The American Cancer Society, 1978.

Levitt, P. M., et al. *The Cancer Reference Book; Direct and Clear Answers to Everyone's Questions*. New York: Facts on File, 1983.

McIntosh, J. *Communications and Awareness in a Cancer Ward*. New York: Prodist, 1977.

Twycross, R. G., and V. Ventafridda, eds. *The Continuing Care of Terminal Cancer Patients*. Oxford: Pergamon Press, 1980.

■ Cancer - Medical

American Cancer Society, Inc. *Cancer Facts and Figures.* New York: The American Cancer Society, 1983.

Beahrs, O. H., and M. H. Meyers. *Manual for Staging of Cancer.* Philadelphia: J. B. Lippincott, 1983.

DeVita V. T., S. Hellman, and S.A. Rosenberg. *Cancer Principles and Practice of Oncology.* Philadelphia: J. B. Lippincott, 1982.

International Union Against Cancer, eds. *Manual of Clinical Oncology.* New York: Springer-Verlag, 1982.

Rubin, P., ed. *Clinical Oncology for Medical Students and Physicians.* New York: The American Cancer Society, 1983.

Schlang, H. A. *Symptomatology of Metastatic Cancer.* Garden City Medical Examination Publishing, 1981.

■ Pain Relief

Parkhouse, J., et al. *Analgesic Drugs.* Oxford: Blackwell Scientific Publications, 1979.

Twycross, R. G. "Relief of Pain." In *Management of Terminal Disease* 1, edited by E. J. Anthony. London: Edward Arnold Publishers, 1978.

■ Children

Binger, C. M., et al. "Childhood Leukemia: Emotional Impact on Patient and Family." *New England Journal of Medicine* 280, no. 8 (February 20, 1969): 414-18.

Easson, W. M. *The Dying Child: The Management of the Child or Adolescent Who is Dying*. Springfield, Ill: Charles C. Thomas, 1970.

Evans, A. E., et al. "Meeting the Problems of Siblings of a Child with Cancer." *Proceedings of the American Cancer Society: Second National Conference on Human Values and Cancer*, The American Cancer Society, 1978.

Futterman, E. H. "Studies of Family Adaptational Responses to a Specific Threat." In *Explorations in Child Psychiatry*, edited by E. J. Anthony. New York: Plenum Press, 1975.

Grollman, E. A., ed. *Explaining Death to Children*. Boston: Beacon Press, 1967.

Gyulay, J. *The Dying Child*. New York: McGraw-Hill, 1978.

Lusk, M. W., and Stephen Hersh. "Modern Treatment of Childhood Leukemia: The Patient and His Family." *Nursing Digest* (July-August 1975): 12-15.

Martinson, I. M. *Home Care for the Dying Child: Professional and Family Perspectives*. New York: Appleton-Century-Crofts, 1976.

Sahler, O. J. *The Child and Death*. Saint Louis: C. V. Mosby, 1978.

Deborah Roth, the author of *Stepping Stones to Grief Recovery,* has been a psychology editor for a women's magazine and director of publications for the Center for Help in Time of Loss. Co-editor **Emily LeVier** leads training programs for hospice volunteers. She has studied with some of the foremost names in death/dying and healing, including Stephen Levine, Elisabeth Kübler-Ross, Ram Dass, and David Spangler. Roth and LeVier are both ordained interfaith Ministers.

ORDER FORM

☐ **PLEASE SEND ME A FREE CATALOG.**

Name_____

Address_____

City_____State_____Zip_____

Quantity	Book Title	Unit Price	Total
	Being Human in the Face of Death *edited by Deborah Roth, MSC & Emily LeVier, MSC*	$9.95	
	Stepping Stones to Grief Recovery *edited by Deborah Roth, MSC* *The Center for Help in Time of Loss*	8.95	
	Gifts for the Living: Conversations with Caregivers on Death and Dying *by BettyClare Moffatt, MA*	9.95	
	The New Age Handbook on Death & Dying *by Rev. Carol W. Parrish-Harra*	9.95	
	Survivors of Suicide *by Rita Robinson*	9.95	
	When Your Parents Need You: A Caregiver's Guide *by Rita Robinson*	9.95	
	AIDS: A Self-Care Manual (Third Edition) *by AIDS Project Los Angeles*	14.95	
	The Law of Mind in Action *by Dr. Fenwicke Lindsay Holmes*	10.95	
	The Laws of Wealth *by Dr. Fenwicke Lindsay Holmes*	10.95	

	Subtotal	
	Sales Tax 6.5% (Calif. only)	
	Shipping/Handling ($2.00 per book)	
	Total Due	

Send Check or Money Order to:

IBS PRESS
744 Pier Avenue
Santa Monica, CA 90405
(213) 450-6485

IBS PRESS
744 Pier Avenue
Santa Monica, CA 90405